Women Living On Purpose

Real Stories of Women
Living with Passion, Intention, and Vision

Powerful You!
PUBLISHING
Sharing Wisdom ~ Shining Light

Women Living On Purpose
Real Stories of Women Living with Passion, Intention, and Vision

Copyright © 2021

The authors of this book do not dispense medical advice or prescribe the use of any technique as a form of treatment for physical, emotional, or medical problems without the advice of a physician, either directly or indirectly. Nor is this book intended to provide personalized legal, accounting, financial, or investment advice. Readers are encouraged to seek the counsel of competent professionals with regards to such matters. The intent of the authors is to provide general information to individuals who are taking positive steps in their lives for emotional and spiritual well-being. If you use any of the information in this book for yourself, which is your constitutional right, the authors and the publisher assume no responsibility for your actions.

Published by: Powerful You! Inc. USA
powerfulyoupublishing.com

Library of Congress Control Number: 2021911177

Sue Urda and Kathy Fyler –First Edition

ISBN: 978-1-7356579-5-0

First Edition June 2021

Self Help / Personal Growth

Printed in the United States of America

Dedication

*This book is for all
who seek to live into their purpose,
share their passions,
and live life intentionally.*

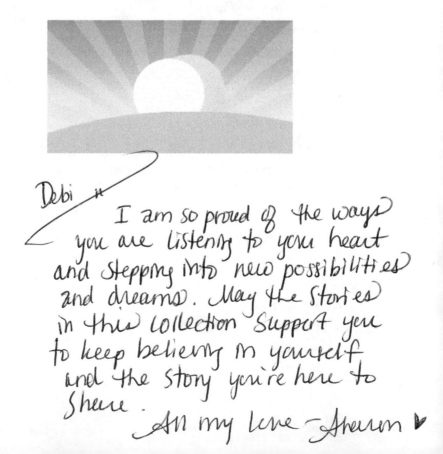

Debi

I am so proud of the ways
you are listening to your heart
and stepping into new possibilities
and dreams. May the stories
in this collection support you
to keep believing in yourself
and the story you're here to
share.
　　　　All my love —Sharon ♥

Table of Contents

Foreword
Dr. Moira M. Forsythe, ND, CPC, PPP

We live in a time of endless shiny new objects seeking our attention, time, and resources but not really adding much value to our actual experience of life. Whether it's the latest technology for business or the coolest new fashion for posting on social media, we have more options than we could ever avail ourselves of in a single lifetime. And yet levels of dissatisfaction with career paths, unhappiness in relationships, generalized anxiety, and even states of serious depression are at levels never seen before in human history.

The return to processes of discovery of deeper core values and ways to live into them is gaining traction as the sustainable method for addressing this internal unrest and restoring connection on a meaningful level.

Studies from several fields of psychology and sociology are showing that as people discover and live into their deepest purpose, they contribute more dynamically to society and culture. Humanity flourishes when we are engaged in realizing ways to express our core essence, outside of assigned roles or expected life choices and more in alignment with our inner callings. Learning to recognize and live into these callings contributes to greater life satisfaction, higher levels of mental health and resilience, and more joy.

I am incredibly fortunate to have had experiences of insight at a young age as to what my "purpose" might be for this current journey of life I am on. I have also been fortunate enough to have had many (many!) adventures along the way that continuously contribute to fine-tuning how I authentically live into that purpose. The relentless curiosity to explore those inner callings has taken me from Alaska to the Appalachians to the Tetons as an outdoor professional, from the halls of Ivy League education in the East to the wilderness peaks of the Rocky Mountains, and from research labs at NIH to executive coaching work around the world. Those adventures may appear to others as ever-changing interests or wild new business ventures but at their core, they are all in service to that deeper mission of sharing my talents and supporting the discovery of inner callings in others, hopefully for the betterment of us all.

"There came a time when the risk to remain tight in the bud was more painful than the risk it took to blossom."
~ Anais Nin

Being willing to embrace the nuances of personal expression as it matures, evolves, and refines itself through experience is one of the gifts we have the choice to give ourselves. Recognizing that doing so is also a gift to the world is a learning that we often tackle repeatedly along the way.

Women Living On Purpose offers the solidarity inherent in the stories of others to support us during those times of challenge when self-doubt and uncertainty might serve to pull us off track from the quest of self-actualization. The women in this book bring a variety of backgrounds, personally, professionally, and culturally, to their processes of discovery. The diversity of experiences belies the commonality of the deeper drive to discover their inner calling and then find ways to bring those callings into more full expression in their lives.

These journeys of curiosity, clarity finding, and courage are each unique and at the same time highly relatable. Discarding outdated paradigms of role assignments requires creativity and determination. Women have always been uniquely equipped with the inner strength to embrace that task but are all too often discouraged from doing so. The many ways in which the women in this book find their way through the distractions and confusion that modern life can bring are inspiring and encouraging.

This book offers many perspectives on what that transformational process can look like and the benefits of engaging with the challenge. Powerful You! Publishing has been committed to bring literary works of higher consciousness to the marketplace for over 11 years. This book is another successful demonstration of their commitment to that higher purpose.

Dr. Moira M. Forsythe, ND, CPC, PPP
Executive Coach, Author, Speaker
Founder: Level 7 Coaching, Creative Leadership Systems
CreativeLeadershipSystems.com/CoachesThatCare.org

Introduction

Storytelling is an art and a calling. It is also a gift, a contribution, a love letter to the world. This book and these authors are no exception.

Most authors came forth open and willing to go to the depths of their personal journeys. They knew their stories could change the hearts, minds, and even the lives of readers. Others came to their stories with trepidation, even though it was on their own that they decided to share their truth in these pages. Interestingly, those who fought themselves the hardest along the way to bare their souls are now content in the knowledge that they stepped forward and unleashed their heart for a higher purpose—knowing that if one soul is touched, any fear of writing or vulnerability in divulging their truth is worth it.

The simple act of stepping into the work and allowing oneself to be vulnerable provides healing for the heart & soul.

Herein lie the stories of 20 incredible women. Many had not considered themselves writers before this undertaking, and they were relieved to find that their truth flowed to the page when they allowed their higher purpose—to assist individuals through their stories—to take the lead.

In talking with each of the authors, we know that the biggest reason and decision to write their story was to help someone else who is searching for answers, someone who needs encouragement and a light shone on the path before them. Many tell of the joy of their transformation or the happy story of how things can work out beautifully no matter the starting point. Others share secrets that they have guarded for many years and, for the first time, emerge from their silence because of the opening, opportunity, and healing that comes along with it. No matter their reason, they each decided the time to share her story is now.

What they all discovered is that an energetic transformation occurs when one puts pen to paper (or fingers to the keypad) with the intent to reveal her truth. As you read each story, you will find yourself feeling the very core of the emotion of the author; whether she is speaking of creating or expanding a business, healing from some sort of tragedy, trauma, or abuse in her life, opening to her inborn gifts and talents, or she is still finding her way to living from her true purpose in this lifetime.

Each transformation is unique and holds its own gifts.

Women Living On Purpose… If you are drawn to the title of this book, you are undoubtedly on your own journey of awakening to a more conscious way of being. You are ready to step more fully into your power and, in fact, by picking up this book, you are already doing it. You have leapt ahead toward your destination and, as you flip through the pages and read the words, you will catapult yourself even further along your own path and purpose. Why? Because we are all connected, and your desire and willingness cannot help but move you forward. The only question is, *will you go forth with ease?*

Are you ready and willing to live fully on purpose?
We believe you are.

Our wish for you is that you commit to yourself to be aware of your calling, your purpose, your joy. Delve into your heart, listen to your inner voice, answer the calling of your soul's purpose—however great or quiet, wherever it shows up, and whatever or whoever is the bearer. Be faithful to your desire to live in and from your heart space. As you do this, you will find your life to be more filled with love, more guided by Spirit, and more consciously aligned with your own heart and soul and purpose.

With deep gratitude and love,
Sue Urda & Kathy Fyler
Publishers
powerfulyoupublishing.com

CHAPTER 1

Self-Acceptance
Heather Keay

As a spirit medium, I know my purpose is to connect people to their departed loved ones. As someone who used to be afraid of revealing my gifts to the world, I also know I'm here to assist other spirit mediums in becoming more self-accepting of themselves and their abilities. There are so many gifted people out there who don't say what they sense, hear, and feel for fear of being judged or deemed crazy. If speaking my truth helps just one of them speak theirs, the struggles I dealt with on my way to self-acceptance will have been worth it.

My journey to recognizing, understanding, and accepting my connection with spirit wasn't an easy one; in fact, I hid my abilities for many years. I was the mother of three young children, and one of my major worries was that people would judge them if they knew about me. Even when I was opening up my own spiritual healing and wellness center, I was afraid to put the word *medium* on my business cards! Looking back now it seems so silly, but at the time I was scared of being criticized and judged, not only by strangers but by my loved ones. Eventually, I asked myself, *What kind of role model am I for my kids if I hide who I truly am?* And yes, there are people close to me who still do not believe in my gifts, but now, instead of being sad for myself, I just feel sad for them.

One of the tools that helped me cope with the reality that I was, in fact, a spirit medium was regular meditation. Though I had always had these abilities, they truly began to blossom after giving birth to my children. Prior to that time I knew *something* was there, but frankly, I didn't care enough to try to learn what it was all about. Meditation helped me understand those abilities, and to deal with my difficulty in adjusting to my new sensitivities and the energy I felt all around me.

I also feared that my gift, which had been dormant for much of my life and now came flooding in, would change my life forever. I remember being on my hands and knees one day, crying and begging God to make it stop and to take all this energy away! Despite my pleas, that didn't happen. Instead, with each growing day, I felt more and more of it coursing through me and around me.

I knew instinctively that I must find a way to release those fears and embrace my mediumship. More importantly, I needed to find a way to empower myself with knowledge so I wouldn't go crazy!

Finally, out of sheer frustration, I decided to educate myself on energy and mediumship. I started devouring every book about spirituality and mediumship that related to my experiences. I spent two years taking classes and workshops to see what resonated with me. I acquainted myself with various healing modalities, visited with mediums and intuitives, and tried to enter each session with an open heart and mind in my quest to find answers. I enrolled in lots of spiritual classes and studied with local mediums to try to understand how and why I'm a channel for spirit. I even went to London to study at the Arthur Findlay College, the world's foremost college for the advancement of spiritualism and psychic science.

Although some of my studies proved more effective than others, I began to recognize that source energy provides me with the necessary ability to *choose* what's right for me.

I realized I was in the process of a huge spiritual awakening, and that there was no stopping it! I found it comforting to know there are so many people out there just like me, and to be able to talk to others about my experiences without being judged. Many of them, I learned, also hid their gifts for fear of being viewed as different.

As I learned and grew, I asked spirit more confidently for guidance and signs. Over time, I began to trust what I heard, sensed, and saw within what I would describe as "moments." Whenever I asked a question, an answer would automatically pop into my head, or spirit would show me something I can only describe as a movie in my mind that conveyed a specific message. I also saw what people looked like and at times even what they were wearing.

Sometimes these messages came without me asking. Sometimes the images provided me with a glimpse of own family members and what they were doing at the same time I was receiving the message from spirit!

As I became more confident with my gifts I began to perform readings for friends, but I didn't tell them the messages were from me. Instead, I said I was passing them along from a medium I had met. This anonymity provided me with the opportunity to test the validity of my gift without fear.

Still, I had to conquer a lot of self-doubt in order to understand and accept that I'm called to a universal mission of great importance. It didn't help that this self-doubt was often reflected back at me from people whom I love and who love me; they simply did not (and still don't) believe in my gifts. Admittedly, this dynamic caused me to question whether my experiences were real.

During this time of questioning myself, I was forced to face some of my own personal demons. The first one centered on the issue of *judgment.* When I found myself in a state of judging others, I would remind myself that this was *their* journey, not mine. It would sometimes take a few days for me to acknowledge this pattern, but once I did I was then able to send them love and compassion.

I spent years of my life hiding who I really am—years trying

to fit into a box in order to be what society perceives as *perfect*.
This never worked, of course, and eventually I came to realize that
I enjoy being different. Now I understand that we're all one of a
kind. Why focus on trying so hard to conform and be like everyone
else, when it's so much easier to realize that there's no one in the
world exactly like me!

For many years, I may have appeared to others to be a happy
person on the outside but I was miserable on the inside. Sad and
empty, I always felt something was missing but could never put
my finger on exactly what it was. It felt like I had a hole in my
heart. Though I always believed in a higher power, I never felt
truly connected.

I meet many people who have no joy in their lives and feel obligated to do things that don't really make a difference in this world.
They spend hours at the gym trying to be a size four because their
friends are thin. They work endless hours and miss spending quality time with their family and loved ones so they can have bigger
houses and nicer cars. As a result, they become resentful.

This is how I felt for many years, but throughout my spiritual
awakening I came to realize that these distractions represent nothing more than an attempt at self-preservation. I now know that my
rush to judgment was a defense mechanism; I was afraid of being
judged by others.

Tuning in to spirit has helped me live a more rewarding and joyful
life. It also offers great protection when I ask for it and helps me to
feel safe anytime, anywhere. Spirit also helps me to heal, which in
turn helps me heal others. In order to do this, however, I must state
my true intentions. I must talk with other people about my gifts.

This is how JLJ Spiritual Healing was born. Deciding to open a
healing center was not done lightly; in fact, it required a great leap
of faith. I set the intention that each and every client who walked

through my door would be healed before leaving. They may not necessarily have fun, but their healing will be profound. I trust always that spirit will help guide us to the root of any client's problems and issues. It's my wish that all clients accept the healing energy and love found in my center so that when they exit my facility, they are lighter, happier, and stronger believers in the power of the divine.

I believe we're all born innocent and pure. However, over the years we tend to accumulate negativity and hang onto our missteps and mistakes, which later become regrets.

Please know that no one lives a perfect life! In order to begin a practice of self-acceptance, it's important to make a full and complete analysis of who we *really* are and who we've become over the years.

The biggest requirement here is complete *honesty.* Needless to say, this can be a very hard thing for many of us to do. When we set aside time to take an honest review of our lives, we're able to identify areas that have held us back.

Facing our transgressions is healing in and of itself—in fact, this can act as our own purification system. Acceptance of mistakes and transgressions is a large part of allowing ourselves to be who and what we are and—in short, *who we came here to be!*

Our relationships is another area that we must look at honestly. We've all either experienced or observed unhealthy relationships —those that cause slow destruction and/or hold us back from our true mission in this lifetime. Some people find themselves in toxic relationships but fail to take action; others go from one toxic relationship to another, wondering why this keeps happening "to them." The truth is that in many cases we are gravitating toward these relationships—and remaining in them for so long—because we lack self-confidence. Sadly, this often stems from early life experiences; many did not experience much love growing up, which makes it even harder to accept love later in life. The first step toward healing yourself comes through acknowledging the nature of these types of relationships. When we become our true authentic selves, external influences can no longer stop us.

Forgiveness of ourselves and others is also crucial to spiritual healing; it also may be one of the most difficult things to master. For many people, giving and accepting forgiveness does not come naturally; rather, many are more comfortable—due to either social conditioning or inherent temperament—trying to exact revenge and clinging to old grievances and the negative memory of those who've harmed them. Even when they think they've let it go, a flashback of the incident occurs and they get upset all over again.

Forgiveness is the key that helps unlock the gates of our own prison. It is the beginning of setting down that heavy baggage we've been carrying. Think about how much more freely we can all move forward if we're not lugging fifty-pound weights behind us everywhere we go!

It also helps to remember that we all endure disappointment, hardship, and pain in this life, and that everything we've gone through in the past is actually by design. Once we do this, we are no longer bound by such restrictions. We set ourselves free.

It's my hope that this message not only resonates with your soul, but sticks with you: we're all special, all gifted, and all possess the opportunity to become increasingly more self-aware and confident at any moment in our lives.

It's human to fear your own vulnerabilities, and acknowledging them can be scary and, at times, very challenging. However, once you release your trepidation, your potential is endless. Do not fear change or judgment—simply embrace the gifts given to you with arms wide-open.

It is easy to become very restless when you're not living up to your true potential. But if you put in the hard work, I promise you'll reap the spiritual *and* earthly rewards. A confidence you never had before will come flooding in! You'll be able to look in the mirror and love who you see—imperfections and all.

Always be your true authentic self, and I promise that you will live a happier, healthier, and more rewarding life. Take off the mask, throw away your cloak, and show the world who you really are and what you are made of! Be the person you were meant to be. We are all unique and we all have something to offer the world!

All you need to do is take that first step...

ABOUT THE AUTHOR: Heather Keay is Certified Reiki Master Teacher, Usui Holy Fire Reiki Practitioner, Advanced Integrated Energy Therapist (IET) Practitioner, psychic spirit medium, and Amazon #1 bestselling author. Heather is also the founder of JLJ Spiritual Healing, located in Cohasset and Duxbury, Massachusetts, where she offers private spirit mediumship readings, group classes, and private and group sessions about how to best connect to the spirit world and learn about strengthening one's own unique, spiritual, and healing gifts. Heather enjoys hiking and looking for signs in nature, especially clouds. She has a husband and three beautiful children and cherishes every moment with them.

Heather Keay
JLJ Spiritual Healing
jljhealing.com
heatherkeay@jljhealing.com
781-424-4073

CHAPTER 2

Disrupting
The Cassandra Complex
Rebecca Saltman

The term "Cassandra Complex" dates back to ancient Greece. As the story goes, the god Apollo was smitten with Cassandra, the beautiful daughter of Priam, King of Troy. He bestowed upon her the gift of prophecy, but when Cassandra spurned his romantic advances, he became furious. Instead of taking away her gift, he did something far worse. He placed a curse on Cassandra so that nobody would believe her prophecies. Cassandra was left with the knowledge of future events but could neither alter these events nor convince others of the validity of her predictions.

A Twenty-first Century Cassandra

This story is problematic for SO many reasons I don't really know how to begin. I will say that the Cassandra Complex has survived millennia and is alive and well in our modern world. How do I know this? Because I *am* "Cassandra." I have spent most of my life being able to "see the future," only to be dismissed or ignored. I am now on a quest to disrupt this story for myself and so many extraordinary women who have amazing gifts of vision and deserve to be believed.

Has finding that "box" you fit in been a challenge for you? You know, when someone asks you that inevitable question—"What you do for a living?"—do you pull something out of the air, like, "I am a professional exotic dancer," because it's easier than revealing the truth? Do you sweat when you must fill out forms that list "legitimate" careers and wind-up checking "Other" (if there is even that box to check)? For me, answering these questions has always been difficult because the words I could use are not used as job descriptions or, more insidiously, are not okay for women to use.

Imagine growing up in the theatre and being addicted to all things science fiction, where anything and everything is possible, then being thrust into the "real" world where having imagination and vision is not only frowned upon, but not listened to or believed, especially from women. Apparently, women cannot be visionaries. Don't agree with me? Name just one famous living woman who is repeatedly called a visionary or refers to herself in that way, because I am unable to come up with one.

HMMM… I just do not think I can accept that any longer.

So, what does all of this have to do with a book called "Women Living on Purpose"? Being an empath, bridge-builder, connector, essential oil hustler, healer, social entrepreneur and, yes, visionary WOMAN has set me on a path to learning skills that did not actually further my true gifts and talents; instead, I had to learn survival skills and become an "expert" in all sorts of acceptable fields in order to belong and fill a job description. I needed to learn how to be a chameleon, navigate my way under, over, in between, and around so I could—as a dear friend put it—"claim my own authority." I even launched a business on International Women's Day called Women On Purpose, for which I interviewed more than fifty women about their life's purpose, never once mentioning who I am and my own purpose. Only very recently did I realize that the way to live on purpose was to come out of hiding and start telling people who I am and what I actually know, whether people believe me or not.

What does the path of a twenty-first century Cassandra look like? Well, I started my work life as an assistant stage manager at Boston

Children's Theatre (a professional children's theatre company at the time) at age ten. Yes, you read that right; I was a big kid so they didn't question me. They only started to question my age when I had not graduated from high school.

I went on to study theatre in college, got a scholarship, immediately went to graduate school to get a degree in producing theatre, film, and television. I was the youngest graduate student in the whole school and often confused with undergrads; it seems I was a bit ahead of even my own time.

Social Entrepreneurship

When I reflect on papers and theses I wrote in high school, college, and graduate school outlining festivals and theatre companies that would pay for their mission by creating aligned business, I realize that today these would have been accepted as social impact or social enterprise ventures. Was this a hint of my "Cassandra" abilities even back then?

I worked in the theatre in New York City and was recruited to work on a most life-changing VISIONARY project: producing interviews with Holocaust survivors for The Survivors of the Shoah Visual History Foundation. In 1994, after the release of the film *Schindler's List*, Steven Spielberg established the foundation to record and preserve interviews with survivors and other witnesses of the Holocaust. For four years I served as a Regional Coordinator, scheduling, coordinating, and connecting fifteen thousand of these interviews from the New York and Boston offices. It was in these years that I became aware of the empathic abilities that allowed me to listen and feel into the experiences of these extraordinary survivors.

I then moved from the world of theatre, film, and television into a more "appropriate" career of fundraising and development. Though there was much I didn't care for, I was pretty good at it and raised lots of money for truly world-changing projects, like the Museum of Jewish Heritage: A Living Memorial to the Holocaust; Huntington's Disease Society of America; and the American Foundation for Suicide Prevention, to name a few. I wasn't good at fundraising for the typical reasons; I was good at it because I came up with disruptive innovations that brought the organizations I was working with new attention, participants, media, and, of course, donors. Many of these innovations were way ahead of their time and would subsequently disrupt me right out of the door.

Right about then, I learned about the idea of social entrepreneurship and thought, *Finally, a box big enough to put all my toys in. Maybe, just maybe, I will even have a box to check!* Social entrepreneurship is, at its most basic level, doing business for a social cause. Social entrepreneurs combine commerce and social issues in a way that improves the lives of people connected to the cause. Let's be clear: though social entrepreneurship has been around for decades most people still don't know what it is.

Quick funny story…My late mother never really knew what I did or how to describe it to friends, so when I was able to give her a term—"social entrepreneur"—she was very excited. One day Mom was flying out to visit me. She sat down and immediately made friends with her seatmate, a business woman flying for work. She asked my mom if she was flying for business or pleasure, and Mom answered pleasure, adding that she was coming to see her daughter. The woman then asked that TERRIFYING question: "What does your daughter do?" to which Mom proudly replied, "She is a Social Entrepreneur!" The woman gave her a puzzled look, then asked, "Does that mean she runs a dating service?" Crestfallen once again, Mom realized she could still not easily describe what I do or who I am, though she did take humor in calling me a modern-day matchmaker.

The Patriarchy & Ingrained Norms

I went to a weekend training called "Success Secrets for the Twenty-First Century" with epic people in the room. They discussed a process they had come up with called "The Harvest," a DEEP dive into people's unconscious competencies, what one does and how they do it. I will cut to the chase—the harvest made me cry because the process was so very intense, and for what it revealed for and about me. When the creator of this process took me aside to discuss it with me, he explained that I was an entirely different kind of connector. He told me I recognized the need to introduce "Suzy to Sam" because I could see that they would do incredible things together IN THE FUTURE, and that my biggest challenge in life would be having the vehicle (business, job, career, religion, et cetera) in which I could utilize this gift. Without that vehicle, I would face the never-ending challenge of convincing Suzy and Sam to trust and BELIEVE me. AND THERE IT BEGINS...being believed. *What on earth is that?*

What's interesting to me, and perhaps the more terrible part of the Cassandra Complex, is that being a visionary is only one small part of her story. As I have seen and experienced, the most painful piece is not being believed. Serious question: why are most male visionaries and futurists believed and women aren't? Is it really just because we live in a patriarchal society where men can do or be anything they want, and women can't?

Let's break down Cassandra's story again. First, the male, Apollo, "gave" Cassandra her gift of vision and prophecy, based on her beauty; second, he turned the gift into a liability when she rebuked his advances. Seriously?!?!? Were Apollo's feelings hurt? Was his ego wounded? As many women are well-aware, we are punished for not meeting men's desires, regardless of our own.

When I think about men's fragile ego, I think about my friend Theo Wilson's poem "Woman: An Ode to the Feminine" (you can find the link on YouTube). In it, he describes a woman being built from scratch: "How strong should the woman's biceps be to cradle a man's ego because nothing is more fragile when dropped back down to earth…The mass alone accounts for 80% of the weight of the world on her shoulders." Funny, right? Yes, because it's true. Women's responsibility is to cradle the male ego, not to take his work away, AND let us not overlook Cassandra getting cursed because she wasn't interested in dating or sleeping with him. So, women have to serve men, or we don't get the good stuff?

Is this curse what has led our society to believe women are less-than? Perhaps this is why "women's work," like keeping house and bearing and raising children, is not considered valuable and is often invisible, and why women's lives often belong to EVERYONE but themselves. Perhaps even my mother couldn't understand my work because she didn't believe me?

Now, for the cherry on the top of this Greek drama: How does an unmarried, childless woman be believed? Our world has a deep discomfort with single women, especially those without children. Why are we unmarried, who did we rebuff, and were we cursed with a lack of children because of it? I assure you I didn't set goals or intend not to be married or have children—quite the contrary. Perhaps I was "cursed," because I had to endure endless treatments and eight female surgeries ending in a radical hysterectomy (*hys*terectomy, a word not lost on me in this story) for fibroids and endometriosis when I was thirty-two years old. I will be clear here—these surgeries and so-called treatments for unbearable pain were some of my most foundational training grounds for overcoming not being believed.

As I was in the recovery room after the hysterectomy and still groggy from anesthesia, I noticed my doctor was standing next to me wiping away tears.

I asked her, "Why are you crying?" to which she replied, "I am so sorry."

"Am I dead? Did you have to amputate a leg?"

She said, "No, you are alive and have both legs."

"So why are you so sorry?"

She went on to explain that she had never seen as many fibroids and such horrible endometriosis in a patient, and she couldn't imagine how I was living with all of that, it must have been awful.

Aghast, I asked, "So you didn't believe me?"

She did not respond, and my inside voice thought, *I hope you will believe your next patient.*

I hope and dream that this day changed her life as it had mine. In the meantime, being an unmarried woman without children is yet another reason for me not to be believed.

Disruption in Progress

There are clear patterns, both in my life and for so many women around the world, and as I write these words I am becoming more and more enraged. What is it going to take for us to start believing and supporting the women around us? There is a glimmer of hope, however…

I thought the world must have tipped on its axis when people started listening to and believing me. A beautiful sister from a different mister from Brazil trusted and believed me when I explained the vision and the opportunity I saw for her. As it unfolded, she reflected back that my vision provided a brand-new career that included her life's passions and a great income for her young family! She has not stopped thanking me for sharing my prophecies with her.

How do we begin to disrupt this complex? I think our first step is listening to and, more importantly, BELIEVING our mothers, sisters, friends, and the other women around us EVERY DAY. If we do, then maybe one day soon we can all benefit from Cassandra's prophecies!

ABOUT THE AUTHOR: Rebecca Saltman is a visionary of change and rabble-rouser for good. She believes OUR big work is to establish a future that is equally distributed and women's voices are critical. Her purpose is to ensure impact where all women are seen, heard, and believed. Early in her career she worked with Steven Spielberg's Survivors of the Shoah Visual History Foundation to ensure that the experiences and bravery of Holocaust survivors was remembered, honored, and believed. Twenty-two years ago, Rebecca founded a social entrepreneurial and media justice organization that bridges the needs of business, government, nonprofits, academia, and media to redefine systems that no longer serve the emerging future.

Rebecca Saltman
Disrupt for Good
disruptforgood.life
rebecca@disruptforgood.life
linkedin.com/in/rebeccasaltman

CHAPTER 3

There's Life in Stagnation
A Midlife Metamorphosis
Sharon Ann Rose

When I was growing up, my mother told me daily about the turmoil, pain, and destruction she read about and saw on the news. Women of her generation were never taught it was okay, powerful even, to feel and be remade by our feminine depths. As a child I presumed it was commonplace to be handed the suffering of the world. "Here honey, can you carry this please?" Trust me, even a small body can hold much more than its size.

My mother lost her father when she was twelve years old. At forty-three he dropped dead of a ruptured aorta while walking to church in the Polish community I'd be born into. His death thrust my maternal grandmother into a world she wasn't prepared for, and robbed my mother of her own foundation.

My father was younger, just three years old, when his older sister, at five, died of an infection in her eye. My paternal grandmother plunged into swelling waters no parent expects to dive into; my father was sent to live awhile with an aunt and his Polish cousins.

Loss, grief, sudden change, sadness, death. They coursed through my blood and history, and settled into my bones. My body worked hard to steady itself beneath their burden; I could feel the significance. Honoring depths of feeling carried me closer to the earth, into a sense of aliveness and connection with life, yet I wasn't comfortable with such a quick and dark descent. It felt like I was being weighted down, unable to move. I learned at a young age to bolster things up, using levity and ignition from inside to lift and shoulder the outer world. I instinctually sensed that this intensity and pain would cause me to become stagnant if I didn't keep moving.

Stagnant (*adjective*)
Without inflow or outflow; not advancing or developing.

synonyms
still, motionless, immobile, inert, lifeless, dead, foul

Tell an Aries girl there's power to be found inside stagnation? Hell no! She'll greet that with brimstone and fire. Little did I know there was a secret power awaiting me, that I'd one day mature into.

Mom's words were like bolts of electricity in my veins. "No one ever taught me about self-love. It wasn't what I grew up with." I was on the phone with her, trying, unsuccessfully, to persuade her to value herself. "The things I do don't matter. They have little value and impact," she said.

At the time I'd hit a tender spot in my growth. I was writing my first book and wanted to access a deeper state of confidence in my wisdom. I believed if I could convince my mother to love herself, I'd restore my own sense of worth and self-acceptance.

My mother's beliefs lived in my blood, right? One must begin at the root.

Raised from the marrow of farmers, I knew the practical and mighty application of digging my hands into soil to find and treat the source of dis-ease. Like a fairy godmother, I wanted to wave a wand over my mother. To travel back in time so I could be born through a living vessel who honored herself and saw how magnificent she was. Worthy of great things even! She'd then pass this embodied experience into all she birthed. I wanted to uplift and transform her self-perspective so I could move forth and live my true purpose, and avoid becoming mired in place.

I was entering the terrain of midlife and could feel a foundational rupture happening. Things were beginning to quake, calling out for attention. I was seeking something I didn't believe I had, and wanted to bolster the ground below me. How else would I become like the shiny silver-haired women I admired—full of their own radiance, power, and conviction? It was either that or follow the trajectory my mother had laid out: "Enjoy being young while you can. Everything gets worse as you get older."

Determined to unearth the mysterious secrets to set me free, I launched a personal investigation, searching every corner of my world with an invisible flashlight strapped to my head. Born with sun and moon in Aries and most planets in visionary placements, I knew I was here for a deeper purpose before I could talk. I listened to inner voices guiding me before I could walk. Instinctively, whenever I felt something try to take me down, I pushed back. Hard. Bringing it higher. I was terrified, deep in my body, of anything considered motionless, immobile, lifeless, or not growing.

Like a heartbeat, I'd always heard a voice inside: "Take care of and carry the world. Hold others up." I was a pleasing child, and felt compelled to do for others what I wanted to have done for me.

Eventually, as I focused on holding and carrying the outside, what lived within became compressed. Symptoms revealed, grabbing my attention. I couldn't carry the weight I used to and keep moving. Old patterns of trying harder, raising everything towards sun and sky, weren't working. There was something beginning to whisper. Inviting me down, into soil. Pulling me close to earth and my body's source again.

It began around the time I turned forty. I was getting ready to birth my third son. His pregnancy was high-risk; I'd developed a blood clot six weeks in and agreed to insert a needle twice daily into my belly to thin my blood. The medical community looked at this condition as life-threatening. I looked at it as stagnation taking hold. Blood wasn't flowing; I was growing "motionless, stale, inert and immobile" inside.

While birthing my boy in the kitchen, I heard the earth speak: "I'm drawing you closer, into your core, so you can feel what rooting and connection in your own body is like. Let me take you down and show you how to let go of the way you've been doing things. May you never leave my center of care again."

This experience asked me to peer at what I'd perceived as stagnation. Holding it with care and love, I began to see what was actually going on and allowed myself to say Yes! to the journey of reclaiming my sense of power and natural flow. Density herself was restoring me. Taking me lower. Bringing me down. Pooling inside, into my base and foundation. Into a settledness in my bones and flesh.

I found great medicine in the settling. In stillness. Being drawn internally. To something that showed me who I am; where I begin and end. It remakes and rejuvenates itself, through this metamorphosis of self-containment and interior sustenance. It's like winter—though we can't see it, below ground there's ancient life and depth—things being fed from inside their being. I'm learning to respect and value this cycle as an inherent feminine rite of passage.

I walk a lot in nature, observing signs and wisdom from flora and fauna. Have you ever seen a stagnant pool of water? It's often teeming with life, richly feeding plants and creatures from inside its ecosystem. In working intimately with women through the transformation of midlife and beyond, I've come to witness the pull from gravity herself, beckoning a new relationship with all we've been taught about our deepest woundings and workings.

As I move through this passage, I feel the call to reclaim my energy, allowing it to recirculate inside my body and psyche. To safeguard me through a period of no inflow or outflow, so I can be with my own experience and wisdom. Here I trace the story of my bloodline, through valleys and switchbacks. To recover lost parts. Clean hidden gems. Find moments when my greatness was taken, given, handed over, swept away. I gather it, day by day, inside my womb, in the cauldron of stillness. Here my blood is changing, completing, growing stagnant, as I rebirth myself into a woman alive and committed to her own self-care, worth, and purpose. In a world that doesn't honor this gathering in or shoring up, who knew it could be my sacred power?

I've been dancing inside this medicine for nearly ten years. Going through seasons of my body closing in so I can restore my wisdom and value. I've learned to move with and through intense cycles of insomnia, migraines, high blood pressure, heartburn, anxiety and panic attacks, excessive bleeding, exhaustion, and hormone fluctuations that take me to the edge of my greatest fear: insanity. Many of my deepest fears have come true. My husband, sons, and I moved from the home we'd dreamt we would live in forever; we lost half our belongings in a flood; and my father became ill and passed away. I've come face-to-face with moments from my past when I was told I didn't or couldn't know myself or own my power, and needed guidance from others or things outside of me. In this gift of midlife stagnation, I'm turning inward to discover my true authority, medicine, and education.

With each wave of my body's change, I become more inwardly still, allowing stagnation to grow. I'm letting it speak up, to push me steadily deeper into this transformation. Through the winter of my being, I feel a rebirth underway—slow, methodical, careful. Even though no one outside can see the process or validate my progress, there's great work happening within. I feel it, replenishing and nourishing at my core.

Like molten lava, the changing blood that once flowed begins to fill me with a new way of being and doing. I dance before the sun rises, caressing my skin as newfound places undulate between my hips. Reserves of energy ready me to go forth into this next creative cycle of outpouring.

My body redesigns herself, from the body of my mother, for whom self-love was so foreign. I no longer spend energy trying to change this; it's what I was born from and can lean into to glean sustenance, capacity, and power. My body and soul feel deeply, and know how to move and carry me through this transition of my womanhood.

This initiation calls in the night, waking me to a purpose and revealing its yearning for me. No longer am I concerned with definitions and presumptions of the outer world. This fire arises inside the folds of my stagnation. It is an ancient vitality, passed down through the women of my lineage, living as a resource within— sustainably, eternally. This is the medicine the earth gives to me. To all of us. It is known in my body and the blood of the feminine.

Like a potter holding clay, I fashion a new form, taking time to tend and bring fresh understanding into shape. To redesign a life I'm being drawn to live, from the desire of all that's swirling inside. From the unknowable, unspeakable place that anchored me to the core of the earth, even before I was born.

"No one ever taught me about self-love," my mother said. "It wasn't what I grew up with."

My blood's stagnation reveals how my upbringing pools inside me. I listen to how it wants to cleanse, clear, and flow through my unique design, into my living, breathing, loving, and dying. Restoring the power and meaning of my life's sustaining purpose.

It was a few years before I first bled. I was ten years old, skipping in the sun along the sidewalk outside my paternal grandmother's funeral. I was smiling, looking up at the sky. One of my older sisters approached, infuriated that I could be happy when our grandmother was dead. I was in celebration of the wisdom of my ancestry, flowing into me. I could feel it.

I turn to that ten-year-old girl now and tell her that one day she'll come to know the power of the still life pooling inside her. It will feed, replenish, and restore her, awakening in some distant time. I put my hand into hers and say, "You can trust the power of your feelings and the purpose of each deep inner change. There's life teeming here. Lean back. Lean in. Let it carry you."

ABOUT THE AUTHOR: Sharon Ann Rose is an author, wise woman and visionary leader who's worked in the field of Feminine Wisdom for more than twenty years. She helps soul-sensitive, creative women in midlife and beyond to rebirth themselves, and reclaim their power, beauty, and lasting legacy. She's the author of *Faces of the Mother: A Journey, A Collaboration, A Feminine Restoration,* and has created several workbooks and courses. Sharon shares one-on-one mentorship, Sisterhood empowerment, and offers retreats across the country. Walking barefoot and staring at the sky are her favorite pastimes. Learn more about her creative artistry and unique care at www.sharonannrose.com.

Sharon Ann Rose
sharonannrose.com
sharonannrose3@gmail.com
503-789-2466

CHAPTER 4

Strength in Heels®
Jami DeBrango-Palumbo

"What do you want to be when you grow up, Jami?" The sun hadn't even fully risen yet and I was already at work, sitting at a long shiny mahogany conference table. I had just turned thirty, was pregnant with my first child, and was exhausted from another restless night. Now my new boss was asking me about my career path.

"I would really like to learn more about Operations." I replied, "I want to be a Site Head, like you."

His response shocked me like a live wire had fallen from the ceiling and zapped me on my backside.

"Well then, you're going to have to take off your makeup and stop wearing high heels."

Wow. I'd looked up to this man, admired his work and experience, and had been excited about meeting him, and that's what I got?

"Well," I said without missing a beat, "I'm not wearing any makeup, and you're going to have to get used to the heels."

He just looked at me—no reply, no movement. I think I wire-zapped him too.

Adrenaline was kicking in, and I was starting to feel a warm flow through my veins. The "offending" heels were clicking under the table, seemingly connected to my quickening heartbeat, like my own rhythmic anthem.

I then stood, thanked him for the "career conversation," and left his office. As I went, my heels click-clicked on the tile—pounded, actually—even faster than usual. Working alongside engineers, you can't help but absorb some of the unique trivial information they like to offer. For instance, I'd learned that I exert more psi (pounds per square inch) when I wear heels versus flat shoes. It also varies depending on the heel. I can exert as much as 1600 psi under a stiletto, whereas an elephant steps at between 50-100 psi. While walking back to my office that morning, I was envisioning that I was stronger than an elephant with every click.

I also felt like I was going to implode. I was the Head of HR for a large biotech manufacturing site, yet at this moment, I felt like the Head of Nothing. The clicking led me past my office to that of an HR colleague. I don't know if it was the rapid-fire clicking or the look on my face, but she immediately knew something was wrong.

"Do you want to know what just happened?" It was more of a demand than a question. Before she could speak, I threw up every word exchanged with my new boss. Then I started crying, and I mean crying. You know, the blubbery, lip-quivering, ugly kind. Through it all my colleague just listened with patience and compassion. It was only when I sank, spent and exhausted, into a chair that she spoke.

"Good for you!"

I looked up, eyes welling again, and said, "What?" Then I added, "I'm never going to move up. In fact, I'm probably going to get fired."

Just then, with precise timing and just the right mix of confidence, encouragement, and conviction, she said to me, "You're damn right—they will have to get used to the heels!"

Within minutes I had calmed down. It was a good thing, too, because I had only a few seconds to wipe my face down and click-click to my next meeting with Inspectors from the Food and Drug Administration. They were onsite for our "Good Manufacturing Practices" inspection, an annual event that could make or break us. The deck I needed to present described the emerging scientific world of monoclonal antibody manufacturing and the people who work behind the scenes every day to make a difference in patients' lives. The presentation was not a typical Human Resources responsibility, but then again, I'd never been very typical.

While educated and competent, I'm really known for two things: working my ass off and for being a "change agent," the latter being a quality I never envisioned as a catalyst for my career. I'd never been the first nor obvious choice for senior leadership roles outside of HR or sales. In fact, until this point, I'd always been a "better fit" in more "traditional" functions. I wonder how many times women have heard the term "better fit" and had no idea what it really meant. It's code for how others perceive you.

After all these years, I know how I am perceived. I certainly do not get noticed because of my stature; I'm barely five-foot-two. I also do not share the scientific-technical pedigrees of many of my peers. In fact, I'm a first-generation college graduate in my family, the first to leave home for school, and the first to leave our home in upstate New York to pursue new opportunities. In summary, I am a short, female, "outsider"; once again, anything but typical.

I moved to California in my early twenties, in part seeking some sunshine, but more importantly, to see what life there had to offer and to see what I could really do. Even as a child, I always wanted more than what was within reach. My mother used to belch out, "We can't afford that, do you think you're a Rockefeller?" Yet with every "no" I heard, my drive only grew stronger. To this day, if someone tells me "You can't do that" or "No, that's not possible," I only become more curious about how to change the "can't" into "can" and the "no" into "yes."

I grew up in a town of Cornhill—this, clearly a misnomer as there was not an ear of corn to be found there, just crowded lower-middle-class homes surrounded mostly by cement. The one park was not exactly for picnics or where kids could explore or play safely. Other than school I didn't leave our dwelling much as my parents told me the "boogie man" lived up the street. It wasn't until later on that I understood that the "boogie man" was, in fact, a drug dealer.

When I was five years old my parents divorced and we moved to a town nearby. It was so small everyone knew everyone, and the majority of its residents were first or second-generation Italian immigrants. It was a different life there, which further fueled my curiosity to observe and listen; it also led me to appreciate and embrace change.

A few months after the infamous day with my boss, I was asked to travel to corporate headquarters in South San Francisco to meet with our Senior Vice President. *Here we go,* I thought, *Am I in trouble?* San Francisco is the biotech industry's hub and the "Birthplace of Biotechnology"—a sea of the most highly recognized global biotech companies, over two hundred of them, working side by side to cure cancer. That thought alone can be overwhelming, especially when you're just a "curious and unassuming little girl" from a tiny town. More than once I thought, *What am I friggin doing here?*

My cab from the airport dropped me off at Building One of the campus, and as I entered the lobby, my high-heels clicked the hard tile floor, causing a few heads to turn. I signed in and showed my badge to security. They took a snapshot of me, gave me another badge, and let me loose into the building. The electric double doors opened, but I had no clue where I was going. Turned out our SVP's office was in Building Seven, and I was in Building One. No problem—my curiosity kicked in, and so did my heels. I was off to explore!

As I walked down the all-white sterile corridors with the prominent DNA helix everywhere. I was so proud to support a new way of making medicine to help patients: monoclonal antibodies, also known as mAb. The antibody is manufactured to bind to substances in the body; the antibody, which is shaped like a "Y", attacks the cancer cells, can block the cells from growing, or dissipate them.

As I aimlessly walked in search of Building Seven, I passed open windows to laboratories with people working in lab coats and safety glasses. There was also a distinct rotten egg-like stench in the air, which meant the cell culture lab must be nearby. At least I knew I was on the right track. The cell line choice we make our antibodies with is "CHO," Chinese Hamster Ovaries. These living cells in media baths behave like teenagers, happy one moment and then pissed off the next, keeping the scientists on their toes.

As I finally came upon Building Seven, I was greeted by a row of artfully-framed vintage biotech tee shirts, each representing a monumental moment in the company's history. What struck me most, though, was the imposing eight-foot-tall framed picture of a beautiful woman. Her name was Helen, and she was gardening. The caption read, "You changed my life, and now I can do what I love." I was so inspired! I took a deep breath, stood a little taller in my heels, and felt ready to take on anything or anyone coming my way.

As I rounded the corner, I saw a row of administrative assistants acting as gatekeepers for their executives. I headed over to the corner cubicle, said hello, and smiled. *Breathe,* I thought to myself, *You and Helen got this.* The woman greeted me in a pleasant voice, "You must be Jami. He's been waiting for you. I've heard a lot about you." I smiled, but inside I was thinking, *Heard a lot about me? What have you heard? Was I late? Did I keep him waiting...? Shit, I'm in trouble.*

The SVP came out smiling, shook my hand, and we went into his office. It was spacious and consistently white, full of lab-like furniture. I sat at a large white conference table eerily similar to the one a few months earlier. On the inside, I felt like I needed a respirator; on the outside, my heels were clicking; thankfully, there was carpeting underneath my feet.

We exchanged some pleasantries and then he got right to it.

"So, I hear you want to be in Operations?"

"Yes, I want to make a difference in patients' lives."

As I said that, I thought of that picture of Helen, and then I started rattling off my performance metrics to show him that I'd done an outstanding job to this point. "My engagement scores are really high, the highest on the site," I told him.

"Yes, I'm well aware. It also seems you have a bit of spunk. We like that around here. If you want to go into Operations, here is what it's going to take..."

I braced myself for his version of "You're going to need to take off your makeup" and wasn't sure if I would reply by giving my notice or by throwing up. Astonishingly, he said, "You're going to need to start in a support group role, perhaps Facilities, to learn your way around the manufacturing floor and learn the equipment, and then build a development plan around that."

My heart skipped a few beats with elation! He then told me that HR had spoken to him and said he was sorry about how I was treated when I initially shared my aspiration. We kept talking, and I shared my plans and long-term vision. I envisioned putting the patients at the center of everything we do, making every decision as if the patients were in the boardroom.

In a blur, our one hour was up. As I was gathering my belongings, he looked me squarely in the eyes and said, "You know I can see you in that role of Site Head. With your spunk, energy, and passion, this can happen, be prepared." As he said that, I walked from around the conference table and he noticed my heels.

Uh, oh.

He said, "Wow, those are some high heels. Are they hard to walk in?"

"No, they're pretty strong." I then passed along the psi theory I'd learned from one of his engineers. "There's strength in heels," I said with a grin.

"Strength in Heels," he repeated, nodding with acceptance,

encouragement, and a smile.

Later, as I waited out a flight delay brought on by the infamous San Francisco fog, I reflected on the difference between the meeting months earlier and the one that day. My voice and my choice of words had made an impression; my curiosity had served me well. The strength of my heels came through!

Two weeks after my trip to San Francisco, I was blessed with a beautiful, healthy baby boy. Shortly after arriving home from the hospital, I got a phone call from my boss. "Hey, there is a decision you need to make. Our SVP says there is a promotion in your future if you want to come up to SSF and be the Director of HR, or you can run maintenance here on our site; that's a lateral move. We need to know as soon as possible."

One of the easiest decisions of my life. "I'll take the maintenance role, and I can't wait to find steel-toed heels."

ABOUT THE AUTHOR: Jami DeBrango-Palumbo is a native New Yorker who now resides in Southern California with her husband Joe, and their two children, Luca and Sienna, and fur babies, Dante and Enzo. She is SVP of Client Services and Operations at Foundation Medicine, Inc., a molecular information company dedicated to transforming cancer care. She is an energetic leader passionate about embracing her strengths and leveraging them for the greater good. Previously, Jami was Global Head of Operations for Sequencing, serving patients all over the world, putting her Strength in Heels® to action. After a tragedy hit close to home, Jami cofounded Kristin's Fund, which focuses on awareness, education, and prevention of Domestic Violence.

Jami DeBrango-Palumbo ~ Strength in Heels®
Instagram at StrengthinHeels1
facebook.com/groups/strengthinheels
linkedin.com/in/jami-m-debrango-palumbo-strengthinheels
Strengthinheels1@gmail.com

CHAPTER 5

Finding the Peace Within

Betsy Lambert

Around seven pm on November 22, 1993, exactly thirty years after President Kennedy's assassination, I was driving my minivan to my gym in Charlotte, North Carolina. The evening was dry, cold, and cloudless.

I was approaching a sharp curve on a residential street at about thirty-five miles an hour when I heard a voice, as clear as if it were coming from someone sitting next to me, say calmly, *"You are completely at peace."* Instantly, I went completely limp as chills ran up from my toes to the top of my head, leaving me unable to move a single muscle in my body.

I was just thinking, *Where did that come from?* when I saw headlights coming around a curve toward me. They swerved to my left as I tried to shake off the paralysis so I could begin braking. Instead there was a screeching crash that sent my van into a spin, then everything went black. I would later learn that I had rolled backward before finally coming to a stop in the woods beside the road.

I had been hit head-on by a drunk driver going between fifty and sixty miles per hour, for a combined force of over eighty miles per hour. Since this happened before most cars had airbags, the only thing that appeared to save me was my shoulder belt and my van's height.

Not that I wasn't hurt. My right wrist had been snapped in two and was dangling from my arm, but though it hurt, it was nothing compared to searing, horrific pain in my legs from the knees down. I couldn't move either leg and didn't know if they were still attached, severely injured, badly crushed, or all of the above.

Then there was the absolute silence of the forest around me that was all the more pronounced after the screeching of the crash. I could see the small, white car of the person who had hit me as bystanders ran to see if they could help. Soon the ambulance came and the EMT appeared but couldn't open my door because the impact had triggered the automatic door locks. I had to grab a long ice scraper next to me with my left hand, then reach across to the passenger side to press the unlock button there so she could begin the process of extracting me. That's when she realized the engine had landed on my legs, pinning me down.

Since she couldn't move me, she cut off all my clothes and placed a Mylar space blanket over me. Still, it was in the low forties, and I was quite cold. I knew if I started to shiver I would go into shock, so I focused all my attention on clenching my teeth to keep them from chattering. The effort distracted me from my dangling right hand and even the pain in my legs; in fact, I barely noticed as the Jaws of Life truck removed what remained of my windshield, peeled back the roof of the car, and put a chain around the engine to pull it off me.

As the pressure eased off of my legs, I looked up and was startled to see stars in the clear night sky. The EMT was then able to cut through the backs of my sneakers so my feet could be extracted one at a time. I was thrilled to find I could rotate each foot, which meant that my lower legs were still attached to my body. As it turned out, the engine wall had pinned the toes of my sneakers and the dashboard's jagged edges had deeply lacerated my legs and knees, but, miraculously, no bones in either leg had been broken.

As they strapped me onto the gurney, all I could think about was arriving in the emergency room and seeing my husband and daughter. The pain was still intense, of course, but so was my gratitude at having survived, and knowing I was going to make it through my surgery and recovery. This is what I said more than once to my distraught family in an effort to console them.

I didn't learn until the police interviewed me that the other driver had been killed instantly. The sadness I felt almost overwhelmed me and will certainly haunt me forever, even though the scant twenty feet of skid marks measured by the police were entirely on my side of the road. Since my temporary paralysis kept me from putting my foot on the brake pedal, the skid marks could only have happened as a result of the collision that sent my car spinning off of the road.

The next morning I was visited by the man who had been in the car right behind me and saw the whole thing. He also happened to be a physical therapist at the hospital where I was taken, and when I told him about the voice I'd heard just before the crash and its effect on me, he said the temporary paralysis likely saved my life. Of course, the fact that I was in a minivan and the other driver was in a compact car had given me a big advantage as well.

At that point, I knew that my life had radically changed, not only because of the crash but because of what I've come to call my "Near Death Experience (NDE) voice." I sensed that something profound had happened to me but I had a lot of recovering to do before its true meaning would emerge. Looking back through the filter of reliving it multiple times and knowing what I do now about how the body functions, I realize that if I had not been prevented from feeling an automatic jolt of fear when I saw the headlights heading towards me I would have reflexively stiffened in anticipation of the collision. This would have canceled out the total relaxation that had been divinely given to me and I would probably have been subjected to far greater injuries, or even death.

Indeed, being hit head-on with such a combined force should have crushed me well beyond my ability to survive. Clearly I had been saved, but why? It wasn't just the miracle of the NDE voice, but the series of events that followed, which I also believe to be miraculous. My heightened sense of the unreality of my situation was so intense that, from just before the crash onward, I often felt more like an observer than a participant.

This perspective began while the Jaws of Life firemen swarmed over my van and I felt like I was watching my rescue from above. I was only brought back to reality after the EMT extracted each of my legs, and the elation I felt as I rotated my feet was almost indescribable. My legs hurt a lot, but they were STILL ATTACHED, something I had questioned up until that moment. At that point I knew I would walk again and that certainty gave me the strength to face whatever ordeal might come.

Since my knees and lower legs were so severely perforated, they could only be cleaned out and repaired using arthroscopic surgery. This left me having to go through painful rehabilitation to get my knees working again, a process that ended up taking almost exactly a year, which was the amount of time my doctor told me it would take. I never knew that muscles could lose the memory of how they were supposed to function, but that is exactly what happened to my left leg. My muscles atrophied due to inactivity while my left knee was healing and quite literally "forgot" how to bend appropriately to allow me to have a normal walking gait.

For the first six months, I had to learn how to function with only one working limb while being forced to live one moment and one day at a time. Though I continued to work full time, I had to go through months of rehab for both legs and my right wrist. My quest for peace during this period had little to do with the NDE voice that protected me during my collision. Instead, it came almost entirely from focusing on my day-to-day struggle and celebrating small successes.

Although I was in good shape before the collision, I was totally unprepared for the challenges of long-term physical rehabilitation. Every step I took with my left leg over that endless first year was calculated as I tried to persuade my leg muscles to cooperate. Meanwhile, my right arm was in a full arm cast for two months and, when the cast came off, my reattached wrist was completely frozen. It would take months of more painful physical therapy sessions before I was finally able to rotate it enough to type and play the piano again.

When an acquaintance said that she couldn't believe I could come back so completely from my injuries, my rejoinder was, "What choice did I have?" When you have a physical challenge of any kind, you simply work through it to find your new "normal" whatever that might be. This didn't take much introspection, just a lot of focused and often painful work retraining muscles to do what used to be second nature.

After a few years, my ongoing discomfort led me to acupuncture to reduce my pain and finish healing my legs so I could begin walking without pain again. If I had not experienced the flow of chi energy from my acupuncture treatments, I doubt I would have been open to pursuing my Reiki attunement and subsequent exploration of other energy healing modalities that I have since come to consider integral to my life's purpose.

I realized after my initial recovery period that my healing process could not be hurried, and, in the long haul, energy healing became an essential tool to deal with my chronic pain. Only after I was successful was I drawn to help others discover how energy healing techniques can tap into the energy of the Universe to facilitate healing of physical or emotional pain or imbalances. I also wanted them to discover their own inner strength, perhaps one they never knew they possessed, just as I had.

I believe that the peace I experienced after hearing my NDE voice prevented me from feeling fear and panic, thus saving my life and getting me through my whole, terrifying experience. The peace I had been commanded to have allowed me to look at my dire situation calmly and in incredible, slow-motion detail. It was nothing like the stillness of meditation, however, but an active, out-of-body feeling over which I had no control, a process that made my consciousness a spectator rather than the driver.

After my initial confusion about the voice I heard, my only reaction on seeing the oncoming headlights was the detached thought, *Isn't that interesting?* As a spectator I solved the problem of opening the locked doors and then calmly told myself to clench my teeth to avoid going into shivering shock. My induced sense of peace and detachment also kept me from screaming in panic when I couldn't move my legs, an otherwise normal reaction that would doubtless have increased my legs' injuries and complicated the extraction process.

My whole focus on peace became sharpened twenty-five years later when I was finally ready to write an account of my experience and its subsequent effect on me. Only then did I discover the forgiveness I needed to give to the other driver in order to achieve the peace I sought.

When the world was forced into quarantine by Covid-19 restrictions, I, like everyone else, had to learn how to look inward for comfort. In my church's Zoom spiritual discussion group, I chose a number that corresponded to a word I was assigned to do something creative with, and that word, not so coincidentally, turned out to be "peace." I will leave you with the poem I wrote for that assignment, which ignited my desire to incorporate poetry into my life, an activity that has now become my passion.

I am Peace.

It starts at my very core, right there next to love
because there is no peace without love.
My peace comes from a lifetime of disappointments, failures,
and ultimate successes
built into of the richly colored fabric my life has woven for me.

Sometimes it seems to slip away,
leaving my inner little girl wide-eyed with panic
that it might have abandoned me for good.
But it always comes back with a soft kiss and a welcoming hug
to calm my soul and reassure me that it never left me.
I had only strayed into the fringes of my consciousness
to sample the imaginary world I think is around me.

My inner peace is my stabilizer and my comforter.
It wraps around me with the softness of a down feather
or a single snowflake.
I recall it whenever I need its soothing balm
to remind me that the crazy world around me
cannot change the magic of Who I Am or who I always will be
- an embodiment of love and, above all, peace.

~ Betsy Lambert, May 2020

ABOUT THE AUTHOR: Betsy Lambert is a writer, poet, medical intuitive, and Body Code Practitioner. When her first grandchildren were born two days apart in 2006, she and her husband Russ decided to retire to become supportive grandparents. The following year Betsy left Corporate America, where she had served as a veteran communications and public relations expert. Her Reiki training subsequently led her to become certified in Quantum-Touch® and the Emotion & Body Code, and she now has a nationwide, phone-based energy healing practice. The 2020 Covid isolation revived her interest in poetry and now many of her poems are posted on her Zoom Poets Society Facebook page.

Betsy Lambert
The Astral Connection
theastralconnection.com
bhlambert@gmail.com
512-757-1669

CHAPTER 6

Path to Purpose
Amber Taylor

I felt like I was drowning, too far out for anyone to even attempt to save me. I was angry, I was terrified, I was frustrated, but when I was asked how I was doing, I always said "Great! How are you?" I was so wrapped up in "keeping up" and "being strong" and not being "the angry Black woman" that I couldn't even acknowledge my own emotions.

It was June of 2020 and there wasn't space for even one more straw on the camel's back. Something had to give. Life was changing drastically, and I felt like I couldn't keep up.

October 2019 – I moved across the country for a new job opportunity

November 2019 – I was introduced to thought work and my first life coach

December 2019 – I became painfully aware of the low point I was at

January 2020 – I started seeing a therapist

February 23, 2020 – Ahmaud Arbery was murdered while going for a run in his neighborhood

March 4, 2020 – Work from Home order becomes mandatory due to the COVID-19 pandemic

March 13, 2020 – Breonna Taylor was murdered in her sleep

April 2020 – I started the certification process for a deeper understanding in thought work

May 25, 2020 – George Floyd was murdered for using a counterfeit twenty-dollar bill

I was working at Microsoft at the time, a twenty-five-year-old Black woman in route to an exec level position. This wasn't by chance, but by grit and determination. I had mastered the art of the "code switch," adjusting [my] style of speech, appearance, behavior, and expression in ways that will optimize the comfort of others in exchange for fair treatment, quality service, and employment opportunities[1]. I viewed it as a necessary evil to achieve success and grew less and less aware of how my ability to code switch was also hindering me from growing into my authentic self and showing up how I wanted to. I fell victim to maintaining the facade I had built for fear that if I let up, everything would come crashing down.

I was so angry I couldn't see straight. I was crying all the time. I was terrified for my husband, my brother, my father, my nephews, my friends, my unborn children. Yet I was still expected to show up to work and produce by my job, my peers, my boss, and myself. But my usual tactics were no longer working. I couldn't compartmentalize. I could no longer fake a smile and generic water cooler conversation. I felt my heart constantly beating out of my chest and this incessant rage bubbling over because I felt as though no one cared. No one skipped a beat. No one took time to acknowledge the state of the country unless they were also Black. It was like suiting up every day for a war fought in silence. It was then when I realized I couldn't be silent anymore.

I started from the inside out—allowing myself to actually feel the pain I was experiencing. I was terrified to let the anger wash over

---

1 McCluney, Courtney L., et al. "The Costs of Code-Switching." Harvard Business Review, Harvard Business Review, 15 Nov. 2019, hbr.org/2019/11/the-costs-of-codeswitching.

me, like if I did, I wouldn't be able to get back in control. I truly believed the internalized rage of myself and my ancestors would be unleashed and anyone in my path would experience the wrath of all of us. But that's not what happened. Allowing my anger to flow actually allowed me to put some space between myself and it. I was no longer anger personified, but a person experiencing it, and for damn good reason. Funny enough, I didn't become some uncontrollable force of emotions, but someone who could have compassion for myself and others who are experiencing them.

This space gave me the freedom to decide what I wanted to do about my anger and the things I believed to be causing it. First, I let people know that I wasn't okay. I wrote a letter voicing my true feelings, concerns, and my ask to the people I worked with. Even though it was pretty well-received and made rounds around the company, the most integral change that letter provided was within me. It was such a cathartic experience to be honest with myself and the people around me that my path went from unclear and confused to the beginnings of an open road.

Next, I got involved with the DEI (Diversity, Equity & Inclusion) initiative within my organization. After the events of the first half of the summer, they created a team with the mission to develop an antiracist culture—without any Black people on it. Needless to say, they needed some work, development, and insight to actually meet the goal they set out to achieve. I took on the leadership role of the initiative and worked with the Black people in my organization to set some lofty goals. These goals were big and scary and required a lot of effort, eyes, brains, hands, and pockets. These goals were not ones we could hit in two quarters, likely even four. But that was the point. Creating a culture of antiracism and dismantling a structure of antiblackness takes strong consistent change and effort across the board. My philosophy was of the belief that if you shoot for the moon, even if you miss, you'll land on a star. Moving the needle doesn't have to be a slow process, but an intentional one.

This work was like an escape to me. It felt so important and reignited my energy in some ways. However, I still felt drained in my actual job. I found myself giving up easier, getting angry easier, and in a perpetual state of loss and overwhelm. This personal turmoil, along with effects of the global pandemic and the state of the country, led me to make a major decision. I needed a break. After talking with my therapist, I applied for a leave of absence.

This leave gave me the space I needed to see clearly. Instead of overworking myself to maintain productivity and a version of myself that was no longer feasible, I gave myself room to breathe. It was only then that I realized that the team I always wanted, the manager who had my back and looked out for me and my future, the job that I wanted, and the salary I dreamed of were not going to make me happy.

It was a hard pill to swallow, but when I looked back at all the things I thought I wanted, achieving them didn't make me feel the way I'd expected, or even good. I realized that I didn't have true passion for the work I was doing, it was more of a passion for doing things "right" and being rewarded for it. My day-to-day job was no longer aligned with how I wanted to show up in the world and the impact I wanted to leave. This realization, along with the idea of the impact I could leave, was the fuel that drove my change.

The Life Coach certification training I was going through for my own benefit suddenly became my light at the end of the tunnel. The work that had been so integral to my healing journey could be shared with others, and I could be the one to deliver that message! I thought of what I needed in my toughest time: a safe space to be myself, my full self, not the one I showed to my coworkers. A place where I could share and get honest, judgement-free advice and feedback without anyone pushing an agenda on me. Being surrounded by people that understood me and my struggles because of their own lived experiences. So that's who I set out to be—as a life coach and as a person in general.

Once I got the idea, I couldn't stop thinking about how to make it work, but I still had a huge amount of hesitation. What was I going to do about my current career? What would happen to everything I'd worked for? Would it all just go to waste? What if I couldn't make it financially? What about my family? What would people think? What if I failed?

For a while, my need to answer these questions kept me stuck. I feared not being in control or having a plan—which is when I realized I was keeping myself stuck because I was trying to control things I couldn't. I was looking for the "perfect time" to even tell people what I wanted to do, let alone plan to actually do it. I was trying to wrap everything in a perfect little bow to avoid the uncomfortability of change and push off the ambiguity that comes with being an entrepreneur. I kept thinking about everything I would "miss out" on or "lose." When I was coached on these thoughts, I was able to see them for exactly what they were—sentences in my brain that weren't helping me get the results I wanted.

My coach helped me see that everything I had worked for was not lost but led me to exactly where I needed to be. I had created magic before, and I could do it again. It wasn't my job, my team, or anything else external, it was me; I am the prize. The skills I learned throughout my education and my career wouldn't be wasted but would be integral to running my own business and being the best coach for my people. I was already exactly who I needed to be, I just needed to trust myself and have my own back.

After that, I took myself and my goals more seriously. I started introducing myself as a Life Coach and coaching everyone I could.

As soon as I graduated my certification program, I launched my website and started my LLC, Amber Taylor Coaching.

I was no longer angry all the time. I was no longer suppressing my emotions for the benefit of others. I was no longer living as who I thought other people wanted me to be but instead who I wanted to be. I had transformed into strength, confidence, and peace in a year where the world as a collective was losing its shit. I could so clearly see that the reason I was able to come out of the fire as a better version of myself was because I had coaching to help me see clearly, take accountability for my own suffering where I could, release myself of suffering that was not my own, and clearly identify what I want and how to get it. Coaching changed my life and it's my mission to help use it to change the lives of others.

ABOUT THE AUTHOR: Amber Taylor is a double Certified Life Coach with the mission to create space for Black women to share, commune, and grow. She teaches them to drop the expectations of others so that they can live in the freedom of their authentic selves. She believes empowering Black women to center their pleasure and joy is the revolution that will change the world for the better. She left corporate America as a Program Manager for Microsoft burnt out and searching for purpose to step into a life of service for others. She is strength, resilience, compassion, and love using her own personal experiences to be an example of what's possible for others.

Amber Taylor
Amber Taylor Coaching
ambertaylorcoaching.com
ambertaylorcoaching@gmail.com
630-301-1826

CHAPTER 7

Being the Gift
Michelle Pesonen

Is this it? Is this all that was meant for my life? These were the thoughts that flashed through my mind as I lay on the filthy bathroom floor of the nightclub. I was also aware of this incredibly empty and lonely feeling, the sense that my life, my very existence, did not matter.

One minute I had been having a great time, laughing and dancing like so many other twenty-somethings in the packed South Beach club. The next minute I was passed out, after sipping a drink someone had laced with the date rape drug "GHB."

My girlfriend was shouting at me "Come on! You have to get up!" as she did everything she could to keep me conscious—shaking me, slapping me around, and making me throw up because she was afraid I was about to die. Finally, in a rush of adrenaline, she picked me up off the floor, threw me over her shoulder, and carried me out of the club to a safer place.

The next day I woke up from the "GHB haze" sick to my stomach. Worse than the nausea was the recollection of what had happened in the club. I felt so violated, horrified, and shocked that someone else could have such disregard for another person's life and try to take advantage of them physically and emotionally.

That experience changed my life and sent me spiraling into a deep state of non-existence. I believed my life wasn't that important. Oftentimes I felt scared, sad, and depressed; other times I felt completely numb, like I was barely breathing and just going through the motions.

Though it was one of the lowest points of my life, it wasn't the first time I had felt such despair. The truth was I had been experiencing these overwhelming emotions ever since the sudden loss of my father when I was ten years old.

I was Daddy's little girl and this little girl no longer had her daddy.

I was heartbroken, and didn't really have an outlet for my grief. I was an only child, and my mom was working two jobs and going to school as she tried to cope with her own loss and pain. Other than school, I spent most of my time home alone.

Always vying for my mom's attention, I would do whatever I could to feel significant—some good…and some not so good. One thing I got really good at was shoving my hurt and emotions deep down inside, which manifested in early adulthood as a debilitating condition called Chronic Fatigue Syndrome.

This would be another very low point in my life.

All the years of unresolved grief, sadness, and loneliness had put my whole being into a state of total exhaustion. All I wanted was to love and be loved, but I honestly didn't know where to turn, or to whom. I knew something had to change, but how?

It got so bad that one night I thought maybe it would be better if I wasn't on this earth anymore. I even began contemplating the easiest ways to end my life.

I thought, *What if I could just fall asleep and drift away? No one would miss me anyway.* Yet, even in that moment I was able to see how debilitating my mind was; how it had spiraled into a place of hopelessness, so deep that my vibration was virtually non-existent.

Somehow, I mustered up the energy to make one last ditch effort, one more shot at some kind of guidance. And I broke down and did something I had never done before: I got down on my knees and prayed. Some pray to the Universe, Higher Power, Spirit, or Source

Energy. That night, as I kneeled in the middle of my one-bedroom apartment, I prayed to God; I pleaded with God to help me.

All of a sudden, I felt this warmth…this calmness. Then a voice said to me, *Go to bed, little one.* That's what I did; and in my pure exhaustion, I knew that somehow…someway…everything was going to be okay.

In that moment…I could actually breathe again.

This incredible experience gave me a newfound energy. I started searching for self-help books, trainings, and events—anything that would guide me to a better-feeling place and where I could be with positive, uplifting people. I had a passion for health and wellness and I loved being the student and surrounding myself with other like-minded individuals. It felt really good to have a purpose again.

As I embarked on this spiritual healing journey, my mind started to open to what was possible for my life. I began reading books like *The Celestine Prophecy,* which helped me see that I wasn't alone, and that there was a bigger force guiding my life. This awareness of a universal energy and source of love forever shifted my perspective.

Synchronicities began to happen and my life started to shift in a beautiful way. Over the next two years, I would meet my future husband, and build a new career in the health and wellness field. I was even chosen, out of everyone in my school, for an award for having "The Golden Hands." What an incredible compliment! It felt really good to be recognized.

Then another synchronicity happened. One of the books I was reading led me to an unforgettable weekend event where I thought I was going to learn about building wealth. Instead, I learned to open up my heart and mind physically and emotionally. I realized there was so much more to this prosperity journey than goal-setting and saving money. I was like a sponge soaking up all the information, and at the same time I was releasing years of pent-up energy and trapped emotions.

It was like a weight was lifted off my shoulders.

I found myself in a space where I was finally allowed to be vulnerable. Though the room was filled with strangers, I felt comfortable and so relieved to be able to expose the tender and raw sides of me. I also realized that there were others who were also dealing with a lot of pain. This weekend of amazing transformation would change my life forever; it was also when I hired my first coach.

Over the next few years, I would meet many other coaches along my path, each taking me to the next level in some way. I attended one of the top ICF-rated coaching schools and even became an associate trainer with them.

I remember thinking, *Wow! You go girl. Look how far you've come!*—never imagining that the real work, the core transformation, wouldn't happen until I met my true light worker and mentor a few years later. My experience with her would be what really turned my life around and ultimately set me free.

You see, though I definitely had come a long way, I still couldn't quite figure it out. I was doing so much work on myself, yet something was still missing. I still couldn't seem to get out of my own way.

I was married to a wonderful loving man, but we would argue and bicker about the littlest things. Whenever this happened I would think, *I'm a coach why can't I figure this out?*

How could I love him when I didn't even know how to love myself?

How could I make someone else feel whole or happy when I couldn't find my own worthiness and happiness?

It was such an incredibly lonely place to be, and a cycle I knew I desperately needed to break. I needed to find the missing link.

This need, this true yearning for an answer, was what led me to Dee. We had actually met some years before in a continuing education class and we instantly clicked. We explored new energy techniques and tried new and innovative ways to test out the hands-on emotional release work we were learning. It was fascinating and I truly connected with her and with the work.

Since then we had done classes together but had never worked one-on-one. Now I kept hearing this voice telling me that I needed to go see her, so I loaded up my car and made the four-and-a-half-hour trip to St. Pete Beach.

As I was approaching St. Pete I felt oblivious to my surroundings. Here I was driving over this massive sky bridge with its enormous strength and beauty, but I saw nothing. I didn't even know how I got to the other side.

I was completely unconscious, self-absorbed, unaware, and so wrapped up in my fear and exhaustion, yet at the same time I had this sense of hope that I was being guided by an angelic force or something even more Divine.

I decided I would surrender and put myself in the hands of the most loving and gracious woman, a light-worker, a gift from God.

As Dee worked her magic, there was an instant flow of love and understanding and that heartbroken ten-year-old little girl was seen, heard, and held for the very first time.

It was such a deeply impactful and heartwarming moment that I could feel the loneliness dissolve, dissipate, and melt away. And simultaneously, I felt this warmth come over me, this peace, this incredible calmness, this beautiful loving energy. In that moment, I felt a sense of freedom for the very first time. This beautiful little girl was finally free.

Later that day, as I drove back over the sky bridge, I was amazed at how different I felt from when I crossed it earlier. I felt like I could breathe and that the blood in my veins was freely flowing again. I also felt this incredible sense of relief, and as I took in the beauty all around me, I knew it was a change that was here to stay.

This was just the beginning of a new leg of my journey. As I started to awaken and shift, I became more present in my life, more consciously aware. I also started to show up differently in my relationships, both with myself and others. I began to be less needy and more selfless while also honoring what I needed. I started to show up in a more loving way with my husband, my family, and the people around me. The release of that ten-year-old girl set me free. This work saved my life.

It was such a gift to be open to receive and feel the loving grace of something so much bigger than myself. To finally find it for myself and give it to myself at any time; to receive it from some of the most amazing and compassionate mentors, coaches, and light workers; and to give it back to those I choose to serve.

I realized that my life is a gift...and that I am "being the gift."

I consciously choose to design my life and do the growth work, not from the space of a wounded little girl but as a beautiful strong woman with a world of love to give.

I am here to tell you that you are never alone. There is a bigger more beautiful lifeforce just waiting for you to tap into it. Your higher power is so much stronger and resilient than you know. There is so much beauty and grace in this world, and I know because I live it every day.

I'm not going to sit here and tell you that every day is roses, peaches, unicorns, and rainbows, but most of them are. I've ditched the drama for a more beautiful existence and I'm blessed with an incredible family, biological and chosen, including an incredible husband who loves me wholeheartedly, even on those days when I'm still struggling a bit.

I'm thankful and grateful every day. I truly have to pinch myself that I get to travel the world, hanging out and working with some of the most amazing peeps, while living my life's true purpose. I am connected to something so much bigger than myself and have the means to do it all—physically, financially, spiritually, and emotionally. I get to do all the things that make my heart happy.

The profound shifts within have brought out a curiosity and empathetic quality that has greatly enhanced my personal coaching style—a blend of traditional and alternative therapies, sprinkled with a soulful spiritual essence.

I am in alignment with the legacy I want to leave, the impact that I want to have, and the intention to be that earth angel to other beautiful souls, so they can see the same light also resides within them. And in each moment, my heart is full.

ABOUT THE AUTHOR: Michelle Pesonen, CEC ELI-MP, is a writer, speaker, and lightworker who is passionate about self-mastery, personal growth, and empowering others to live their best life and leave a legacy of pure positive impact. She is a Certified Professional Coach, Energy Leadership Master Practitioner, and the creator of the Heal, Manifest, Flourish Signature System. Michelle loves to bring a divine spiritual essence to her coaching, and combines alternative modalities such as NLP, Emotional Release, Touch for Health, Dream Sculpting, Timeline, and Angel Guidance, which enhances her traditional coaching practices.

Michelle Pesonen
The Conscious Coaching Experience
healmanifestflourish.com
michelle@hmfcoaching.com
954-607-2580

CHAPTER 8

Living in Alignment

Understanding It Is Not Always a Straight Line!™
Donna W. Woo

“**I**know I must have a purpose. I must be here for some reason. What am I *supposed* to be doing? Shouldn't I be happy with all the goals I have already accomplished? I thought I'd finally found my life's calling and was living it, so why is something still gnawing at me?”

I've asked myself these questions throughout my life, but recently my inner voice has been speaking to me louder and more frequently than ever. It does not make sense that I feel out of alignment; not in line with my higher self; or "off." I have worked so hard to get where I am today. I even survived my own birth! My mom told me she tried to abort me three times, yet here I am!

The Aligning Path to Becoming Dr. Woo!

It took me over twelve years to become a chiropractic physician, and oh, what a struggle it was to get there. I was an honor student and awarded scholarships for college, but I had given them up to move out of state and marry my first-and-only boyfriend about a month before my twentieth birthday. I knew I was going to be successful in my future, but because of my low self-esteem, I did not want to be successful and all alone. Well, after almost four years of marriage; moving several times; getting an associate degree in small business management; and having many odd jobs, I wound up divorcing my husband and moving back home with my mom.

It would take me nearly eight years, but I finally graduated with my bachelor's degree in athletic training and a minor in biology. It took another four years to graduate from chiropractic college. Then, because of the rules in Nevada at that time, I had to wait almost a year to get licensed. While waiting to pass the state board exam, I worked about five part-time jobs at the same time, including being an adjunct anatomy professor and a shoe model! I also got licensed in California and Utah, which enabled me to do some chiropractic work at my friend's office. This was the first job I absolutely loved and, unlike many other temporary jobs, where I could not wait for the assignment to be over, I wanted to keep going back for more!

Coincidentally, about this time I saw an eighty-seven-year-old female chiropractor on television who was still adjusting patients! I thought, "Wow! I will be able to practice forever! I've finally made it to my true calling!"

I could write a whole other chapter on finding a place to practice. Let's just say that process was also filled with twists and turns, including moving four times; getting loans; spending hundreds of thousands of dollars; engaging lawyers; receiving support from great friends and family; and building out *two* offices from scratch. When I was eventually able to purchase my own office in upscale Summerlin, I *really* felt this was forever and that I would be safe and practice there for the rest of my life! As of this writing, I have been practicing for over twenty years and have helped thousands of people who initially thought there was no hope.

Help! I Think I Need an Adjustment!

Some people would think I was crazy to even think about giving up my practice after I had spent so much time and effort to achieve my dreams. The truth was, I was burned out, not only in business, but in my personal life. Then Covid hit, and I used the "pause" as an opportunity to close down most of my practice. I told myself I would take a one-year sabbatical, then reassess my situation.

Well, the Universe didn't wait that long. A few months ago, my neighbor approached me, unsolicited, and offered to buy my office! Selling is a huge step, requiring me to take bold, uncomfortable action, but I am opening myself up to new possibilities. For the past year, I have been taking classes to hone my skills as an inspirational speaker, mastermind facilitator, and author—all of which I believe is part of the Universe's purpose for me. The sale of my office is happening as I write this, and is set to close on my birthday, which is next month—another "coincidence"!

Another reason I have the courage to make such a big change is the stress I observed in my patients. Many of them were executives, business owners and their families, but though they fit the traditional definition of success they did not really seem like they were enjoying their lives fully. They were doing what they thought they *should* be doing, rather than what they truly desired. I know people have the potential to live beyond the "shoulds." By speaking and writing, I really want to help them see that potential and bring more joy to their life, but I also want to practice what I preach.

It's All Connected!

Self-Love: Although I'd been working on my own self-development for decades, I got burned out because I did not truly love myself and was not comfortable in my own skin. Last year, as a milestone birthday approached, I decided I was going to finally achieve this as a gift to myself. I focused on my inner work, such as learning to speak up for myself; learning to trust my intuition; and joining groups with like-minded people. I also had to tell myself that I am nice and kind and it is okay to be powerful. I truly believe the key to success and joy is loving and having a great relationship with ourselves first. When we are in alignment with ourselves, it allows us to have better relationships with everything and everyone. We also take better care of our health; we have greater wealth; we can be useful to others; and we can have more fun! (I also believe it leads to world peace!)

Health: My grandma always said, "Without your health, you have nothing." I plan to live to be one hundred years old, but I never know what the Universe has in store for me. My mom was diagnosed with cancer at the age of fifty-eight and fought courageously for six years; my aunt started getting noticeable dementia in her late sixties; and I had my own health scare a few years ago. I frequently hear people say, "I am going to die anyway." Yes, it is true, but what if we live longer than expected? Do we want to live in a nursing home, or do we want to live independently in our own home? I intend to do whatever I can to have the second option! Again, when we love ourselves, we also make healthier choices. For me, this includes a life change that will allow me to live more fully, rather than remaining "stuck" in my office and possibly spending the rest of my life in regret.

I am also learning to focus on my health within my marriage. My current husband and I have been together for twenty-four years and married for nearly eighteen. He is handsome, smart, and funny, but he does not always make the best choices for his health. I have been trying to help him, but he does not always want that help. It was as if I were living a double life—I could help people with alignments at my office, but I was having a difficult time being in alignment at home. These days, I am working on establishing healthy boundaries so his decisions, while important to me, do not affect my wellbeing.

Wealth: I realized during this journey that I was also out of alignment with regard to financial abundance. I had a really poor relationship with money, due to the many mixed messages I received while growing up. More than once we had our utilities shut off and our cars repossessed because of my dad's gambling, which made me fearful and feeling like I had to work really hard so that never happened to me. My grandparents also cut my mom off financially when she married my dad, and my grandma never seemed happy despite her wealth.

Being in a helping profession, I was often conflicted about my fees. I needed to cover my overhead but felt guilty for charging more. So, although I was able to make a good living, I really had to work my "anatomy" off, not just so I could provide great service and value to patients, but to meet my own bills.

I have learned that the lack of money is not honorable; it just made me cranky. I've also learned that the way we think about our finances is often a reflection of our self-worth. When I love myself, I have the courage to charge the fees that are commensurate with the services and value I provide. This in turn helps my health and also makes me a nicer person in the community.

Being Useful: Two other beliefs that keep me in alignment and on purpose came from my grandpa and my mom. Grandpa always reminded me to be "useful," and I want to make sure he is proud of me and of my mom for raising me.

Having Fun: My mom said I always worked too hard. I was trying to work hard so I could live a life of choices. She was the one who reminded me to have fun, and that life is to be enjoyed too. Today, one of my goals is to balance Grandpa's advice, to "be useful," with hers, to have fun and freedom.

It Is Time for Another Adjustment!

I used to believe I just had one purpose; now I realize my purpose can change and I can take several paths in life. Being in alignment is also not always a straight line. In chiropractic, shifting the spine and joints into alignment allows all the other parts to communicate with each other. This in turn, helps the body heal itself and function better!

As stated earlier, I believe the key to living a more joyful and well-rounded life is being aware and intentional, especially in the areas of self-love, health, wealth, being useful, and having fun.

When I look back, everything I accomplished started with the setting of an intention, including completing my formal education; owning my office; being debt-free; staying healthy; staying married to my current husband; and learning new skills so I could help more people while being useful and having more freedom. Yes, I did whatever I could to make it happen, but the Universe always stepped in to help.

I have also learned to listen for signs the Universe is sending me. The other day I heard on the car radio the story of a man who sold his medical practice, which he'd had for seventeen years, to go help his brother in the ministry. Like me, the man had gone to school for twelve years. The speaker telling the story said in the ordinary it made no sense. This may be true, but after hearing it I was more comfortable selling my office.

It is also interesting that when I first started my practice, I attended a work event with one of my friends. There was a fortune teller there who told me that the job I was doing was only temporary. I did not really believe her, but I remembered what she said.

Also, recently, I was in a challenge with over one million people and one of the participants put a post looking for the "pom pom lady" because of her great energy and the joy she was bringing to the group. That "pom pom lady" was me! This was validation that the world appreciates me sharing my joy!

The Adjustment Is Holding, For Now….!

Sometimes I feel purpose is a struggle between what we think we *should* be doing and what we *want* to be doing. I struggled with knowing my purpose and believed I found it because I'd worked so hard to become a chiropractic physician. I defined myself by my career. When I got to where I wanted to go and had everything I thought I wanted, I felt something was missing. Did I want something more or just something else, or both? I felt obligated to keep doing what I was doing because I was afraid to let others down; did not want to be judged for being lazy, not useful or living up to my own potential, or stupid. I was also conflicted because I wanted to be helpful to others, but felt it came down to a choice between my own life/health and theirs.

I have learned to have courage to make bold moves; to be myself and not be afraid to say and do what I want; to listen to myself; put plans out to the Universe; and to love myself in support of my health, wealth, usefulness, and joy. This in turn will change the world!

I am a woman living in alignment, understanding it is not always a straight line! I am a woman living on purpose!

ABOUT THE AUTHOR: In over twenty years as a chiropractic physician, Dr. Donna W. Woo helped thousands of patients, including professionals, executives, other doctors, business owners, and their families. She noticed that their stress levels, desire to please people, and not living life intentionally often contributed to their pain. When she too became burned out personally and professionally, she took a "pause" and allowed the Universe to lead her in an exciting, new direction. As an Ambassador of Happiness, her main purpose now is to inspire and help people live with intention and cultivate their relationship with themselves so they can create a life of abundance in health, wealth, usefulness, and joy!

Donna W. Woo, DC, LAT, ATC, CCSP®
Donna W. Woo Media Ltd.
DrDonnaWoo.com
Donna@DrDonnaWoo.com

CHAPTER 9

The Sensitivities of the Horse
Lois Winters

Finding my purpose has been a life-long search, maybe because I did not follow my intuition for many years. I remember always enjoying animals, even as a child, and whenever we visited a farm I was off to the barnyard to see whatever I could find. We had cats or dogs, but I always wanted a horse and envied the kids from the farm who had those majestic animals. As an adult I went to see the Lipizzaner Stallions perform and their beauty brought me to tears. Never did I imagine I'd be working and living with horses later in life. I also had a passion for encouraging and empowering others, but I felt very inadequate as I could not even empower myself.

Twenty years of marriage came to an end when my husband disclosed that he had been arrested for hiring a prostitute for the second time. It had started several years earlier, when he revealed he was a sex addict, shattering my understanding of family, as well as my self-confidence. I questioned if I had failed him in some way—perhaps if I had been the perfect lover, he would not have felt the need to stray. I judged myself for not seeing the signs that now seem so obvious. I lost all confidence in my appearance, skills, intelligence, attractiveness, and value as a person. Despite my own depression and anxiety, I supported his treatment while feverishly working to improve the way I behaved, looked, and spoke. Now, suddenly, unexpectedly, I found myself alone. At first I was so happy to be free of the control I had allowed to shape my way of thinking, most of my decisions, and my self-worth—or lack thereof. But soon, all the emotions I had been suppressing for the past two decades surfaced with an intensity that brought me to my knees.

Some of my efforts to "revamp" myself yielded positive results, and I'm grateful for the push to become more independent and learn about who I really was, rather than defining myself as a wife who did not measure up. I took classes, did volunteer work, went to counselling and read many self-help books, and searched for a career where I could be myself, but I could still not put my finger on where I belonged.

When my marriage finally ended, the anxiety that had plagued me most of my life became overwhelming. I prayed for the pain to end, even if it meant leaving this life. I finally went to see my doctor, who gave me medication that saved me. Eventually I started dating and having some fun—maybe a bit too much fun! I also kept looking for a career that would fulfill me, but it continued to stay just outside my grasp.

It was through friends that I met Vince, a handsome cowboy who also farmed, and I fell head over heels. He lured me out of the city, where I had lived for most of my married life, and for the last twelve years I have lived in the country with him and our fifty horses, three dogs, and three cats.

Truth be told, I found the transition from city to farm life a bit tough. There was so much mud! So much work! We also shared an old house with Vince's elderly and very Catholic parents, which was an adjustment in and of itself.

I'd had a limited amount of exposure to horses before I moved to the farm, but most of it was not good. Over the years I had been kicked in the hip, run through a fence, bucked off several times, rubbed off, and chased out of the pen. I still loved horses, but I also feared them. Many of Vince's horses were not trained to the halter, which meant that for me riding was out of the question. I did spend time learning how to handle them, though, and soon I was treating horses that were injured and quieting the newborn foals.

At this time, I was working in the city an hour away and not enjoying my time there. I decided to leave and work on the farm for the summer while I searched for something else. Whether by luck or divine intervention, I came upon a course for teaching equine-assisted learning—a process where horses help people learn life skills. There is no riding involved, which surprisingly enhances the horse's ability to teach. I signed up for a weekend program to see if this was for me, and just like that, I finally found my calling! I signed up for the six-week program, after which I was hired for a position as an equine-assisted learning facilitator at a brand-new facility in a local First Nation community. It was a huge learning curve for me as I'd never had much exposure to First Nation culture, nor had I worked with horses and children on a daily basis. That wonderful experience led me to a level of personal discovery I'd never expected, as well as a new understanding about human nature, the impact of trauma, the healing processes, and the importance of continued growth.

Because horses are prey animals, they have a heightened sense of movement, exceptional hearing, and a keen sense of smell. Their eyes are on the side of their head to allow them to see almost completely around their body, but they do not have the depth perception we do and cannot see in as much detail. This can cause them to spook easy, especially if they are young or inexperienced. They are constantly on the watch for danger, and their first line of defence is to run away. As humans are considered predators, horses have a natural wariness of us and are always on the watch for aggressive behaviour. They can sense if we are angry, scared, sad, happy, or calm, and will react to the emotional and body language we display;

this opens a window of opportunity for meaningful connections between horses and humans, along with some incredible and important lessons.

One incident that stands out in my mind involved a young lady in our adult class. She had come from a difficult background and clearly displayed the results of trauma. On this particular day, we were starting the students out slowly by letting them walk among the horses, observing and interacting with them. The young lady was very nervous, so she was standing off to the side when one of our horses, Bobby, slowly walked up behind her and put his head on her shoulder. This was an amazing moment. Bobby had also been treated poorly in the past. When he first came to us he seemed totally tuned out and lacking in personality, but with time and care he came out of his personal prison and showed us what a wonderful fellow he was. Still, he often avoided people and had never approached anyone like this (nor would he ever do so again). This touched the young lady very deeply, and they had a bond from that day on. Over the course of the year she attended these classes, her confidence and communication skills grew, bolstered by her relationship with Bobby.

We also held workshops for companies and organizations, with very interesting results. One manager discovered that when she treated the horses in the heavy-handed, aggressive way she did her staff, they did not respond well. This encouraged her to do some reflecting on her management style, and to admit her shortcomings in order to make changes.

My work at the centre also started me on my own path to healing. I realized that I have a level of sensitivity and empathy that can make life painful. I had buried it over the years to stop myself from feeling this pain. I also had a tendency to become anxious, often without realizing what triggered it. When this happened, my actions were often fast and I was not in touch with what was going on with the horse or the participants. As a result, the horses would move away from me or not cooperate with whatever I was trying to do. Through observation, I began to understand that what was going on inside me was affecting these wonderful animals. I couldn't just hide how I was feeling; the horses saw right through my act and wanted very little to do with me. I watched this scenario play out over and over, both with myself and with others, and it was always satisfying when the human figured it out and modified their behaviour, then saw the horse respond in turn.

Unfortunately, that equine facility closed due to funding short-ages; however, my experiences and learnings are just beginning. A few days before I sat down to write this chapter, I stood in the pen at our farm with one of our colts, feeling frustrated and at a loss for what to do next. I had been working with this fellow intermittently throughout the summer months, attempting to quiet him enough to put a halter on him and prepare him for accepting a saddle. Even with my experience, I was struggling—one sudden move and he was gone. I asked the Creator for a teacher, and one came to me in the form of an audio book by a young female trainer who used a method I felt more comfortable with than any I had previously come across. I then found a book that taught horse behaviour and handling through the story of a young man learning these skills from a brilliant, gentle, and very effective old man. These books shifted my perspective and gave me new ways to approach this challenge.

The next day, I went to the pen brimming with new knowledge. I had been reminded that he was a sensitive horse with very little confidence, and he needed my patience. Then it hit me: I had not been patient with him, or with myself! I was pushing him harder than I should have been, and had been putting so much pressure on myself for not being farther along in my classes. Neither of us were learning as fast as we could have been because all my energy was going into thinking that I should be more or different instead of just being okay with what is. Once I slowed down and took the pressure off him, I began seeing much better results and the horse is now easy to halter and lead. And once I eased up on myself, I began feeling calmer, experiencing less fatigue, and thinking more clearly and creatively. I ended up learning just as much from this young horse as I was teaching him, if not more.

I am still on the journey of self-discovery that took off during my time at the equine centre. One of the biggest steps on this journey has been recognizing the source of my lack of self-confidence and self-esteem. My parents came from challenging backgrounds, leaving them both with confidence and communication issues, as well as depression. My siblings and I never lacked for care and always felt that we were loved, but our parents could not teach us what they did not know. As a result, I struggled for a long time with confidence, with being able to speak my mind, and with standing up for myself or even figuring out who I really was. In addition, an incident of sexual abuse at the hands of a stranger when I was around four or five years old (I did not remember this until my adult years) likely contributed to me turning off my emotions as a child. There were a few difficult situations during my life when my feelings and awareness surfaced so strongly that I had a very hard time coping. One counsellor decided I had PTSD, which was triggered at difficult times. And on top of all of that, my first marriage and subsequent divorce had left me feeling very inadequate in many ways.

It took me many years to find my calling, but now I cannot imagine a life that doesn't involve working with horses. The acceptance and love expressed by these animals is very powerful. I relish my time learning with them, laughing at their silly antics, brushing them over, giving them hugs and kisses, and breathing in that special horse smell. Even though some of my experiences with them have been difficult, and still are at times, I am very grateful for these challenges as they have given me a heightened sensitivity to people's feelings and a desire to understand how and why people, and animals, do what they do. My sensitivity and empathy is much freer to be felt and expressed, which then allows me to help others. And when it becomes too much, I have my special companions, the horses, to bring me back to myself.

I now know that helping and empowering others is my passion. This world of helping and healing is exactly where I want to be, and the horses are the perfect companions for this role. I have learned so much from them over the past twelve years, and I look forward to learning even more in the years to come.

ABOUT THE AUTHOR: Lois Winters became an Equine Assisted Learning Facilitator (EAL) after years in the business world and knew instantly this was where she was meant to contribute. She is also a natural caregiver, being her husband's home hemodialysis assistant, caring for their horses and dogs as well as helping at the carehome, where she does the bookkeeping. Her caring personality is a perfect fit for an EAL program; however, the facility where she worked closed. Her long-term plans are to eventually start a centre or assist at an existing centre. She is also developing an online course to guide people using home hemodialysis on the transition to a whole food, plant-based diet.

Lois Winters
vldenis@baudoux.ca
306-227-6962

CHAPTER 10

There is Always a Way
Klara Brown

Divorce can be an earth-shattering experience, especially for those who didn't see it coming. Some feel blessed by having the courage to move beyond an unhappy, unfulfilled, or even an abusive relationship, while others are devastated by the loss. Either way, it's a major interruption in life. I know what it is like to lose trust in yourself or in others, to feel unsure of who you are. Life becomes uncertain and you don't know how to move forward. After two failed marriages, I *do* know what it takes to redefine yourself and rebuild a happier and purposeful life.

Is this real? Is it really happening?

I stood in front of the spiritual teacher and long-time friend who had conducted our wedding ceremony. The room was beautifully decorated in a Buddhist tradition with flower arrangements overflowing on the floor. The place was packed. Some people were standing because no more chairs were available. My daughter was sitting in the front row. I sensed her presence. On my right side was my maid of honor, a dear old friend, and on my left was my future husband. My face was burning up and my body was tense from nervousness. My vision was blurry, and I was trying to hide the tears flowing from my overwhelming emotions. When I said "I do" to my marriage, I said "yes" to a new chapter of my life.

I was a fifty-six-year-old professional, successful woman getting married for the third time. I felt gratitude and grace enter my heart as a warm feeling streamed forth into every cell of my body.

Split World

I grew up in Hungary. At an early age I witnessed my parents' anger, blame, and unkind behavior towards each other. They were the products of poverty, abuse, and the impact of World War II. They both carried deep emotional scars. Then the Hungarian Uprising brought more pain to our whole family. The year 1956 is one not easy to forget. I was four years old.

The chaos began in the capital city where we lived. We stood in front of the window, watching the unimaginable. The building was in flames, burning our eyes and forcing us to evacuate. On the street, people were running without clear direction, while tanks rolled down the main road, followed by men holding firearms and shooting aimlessly at others. My father shouted at my mother to take me away from the window, then he pushed us out of the apartment and down to a basement where other tenants had already found refuge. I could feel the horror and confusion of not really understanding what was really happening. My mother grabbed my hand and literally pulled me to move faster. I heard my father's voice, "I will catch up with you soon," but then we didn't hear from him for a few days. Everything was so surreal as I tried keep up with my mother. I needed her reassurance and comforting words, but she did not say anything.

Decades later, during a seminar event, I processed this experience. I realized that I had been looking at the world through four-year-old eyes for all those years. My trust had been violated by my mother, who was supposed to protect me, comfort me, and keep me safe from violence. Since that incident I felt that she didn't love me or even care about me and that it was probably my fault. I become an angry, rebellious child, learned to distrust, and expected betrayal while growing up. This rippled throughout my life in many forms. I was an only child. I never felt that I belonged or was enough. To compensate for my pain, I created my own world where I felt safe and protected from harm, and allowed my imagination to run wild.

I was a smart kid and at six years old I learned to read in a short time. Nights were my favorite time. After my parents fell asleep, when everything quieted down and the darkness hovered over my room, I would hide a small lamp under my blanket, pulled out my favorite fairytale, and read for hours. The stories were all about heroes—the challenges they had to face, like finding the golden egg that the dragon protected. My heroes were fighting and winning over enemies and mystical creatures. At the end, they earned the princess' hand, and the kingdom. I fell asleep happy and dreamt that beyond pain and suffering there was a magical life that could be reached.

My world was split. My inner world was full of wonder and curiosity, eager to be shared and recognized. My outer world was dangerous, scary, shameful, and judgmental.

To my father, I was a "Shining Star"; however his behavior was unpredictable. There was no trust in that parental relationship either. I kept many secrets of painful events that I was not able to share with anyone.

My relationship with God was also broken. I was told that God sent mothers, who did the work for Him. He loved people who were good, but bad people were punished in a "unique" way. I was sure I was the latter.

The person I trusted most while growing up was my father's sister, but I still couldn't be totally open with her about being molested and raped at a young age. I thought I might eventually have the courage to reveal to her my shame, but she died before I could do this. Her leaving this world left me with a deep-seated loneliness.

Distrust has a significant impact on human relationships. Without trust, there is no intimacy or love. When conflict arises, we either avoid it or feel constantly in its grip.

What is trust? We learn from past experiences to determine

who we are today and how we relate to each other. We might tell ourselves, "I am scared to get hurt by entering into a new relationship," or "I have to protect myself, and be emotionally withdrawn."

The spiritual teacher Osho once said, "Trust is a quality in you… Trust is your inner growth…Trust is certainly a higher value than love…Trust cannot be without love. But love can be without trust, and a love without trust is ugly; deep down it has all kinds of jealousies, suspicions, and distrust."

When trust is deeply violated, we first lose trust in ourselves. We believe something is wrong with us because otherwise the people who harmed us wouldn't have done so in the first place. Regaining trust in myself and others has been a process in my journey. The mantra "There is always a way" became my resource to fight for a better life. I sought answers for these questions: How can I improve my relationship with the phenomenal world in which I am immersed? How can I have joy and happiness and make the world a better place to live in? The answers didn't come right away or in a comfortable way. They came only after more challenges, more mistakes, and more failures.

The Journey

I was thirty-three years old. My second marriage had just ended. At that time, I lived in Charlotte, North Carolina. I thought I could leave behind an unhappy, unfulfilled relationship and I would be happy again. But the truth was, I was still unhappy. I buried my feelings in long hours of work and boring relationships. A few months later, I slipped into a major depression that damaged my relationship with my daughter. The pain was unbearable. I felt embarrassed, angry, scared, cut off from people, and very lonely.

Have you ever experienced being so hopeless that you just want to give up?

Then I got hit with this thought: "What if there is another way?"

I couldn't shrug off this feeling of hope. I prayed for a solution. I still remember that moment when my life changed forever. I was sitting in my small apartment. From my room I was watching a beautiful sunset descend from the sky. But my room was getting darker, and I felt the weight of the world crashing in on my heart. The phone rang. I picked it up. On the other line was an old friend's cheerful voice saying, "Hey, I am going to a meditation retreat for the weekend, and you must come. I will pick you up in an hour." Then she hung up the phone. I knew this call was the answer to my prayer. My daughter was spending the weekend with friends, so there was nothing to hold me back from going.

In meditation, we make friends with what we reject, with what we see as bad in ourselves and in other people. We develop this attitude by practicing mindfulness. Sitting on a cushion or a chair, we see our thoughts rise, we touch them, and then we let them go without judgment. Meditation practice helps to cultivate a different attitude toward the unwanted elements of life. If something is painful, we become willing to not just endure it but to let it awaken our heart and soften us. Whether we are experiencing pain or pleasure, we let our experience be as it is without trying to manipulate it, push it away, or grasp it. We are accepting ourselves without judgment. It is not a thought; it is more about seeing clearly and letting things be. During meditation, we let ourselves see what is happening, whatever it is. In mindfulness meditation, true compassion naturally arises.

I left the weekend with a heavy load lifted from my shoulder. By the next day I was free from depression.

I was fascinated and curious about what had happened to me over the weekend. I became obsessed with learning more and understanding the human mind. How can one learn to use their thoughts to shape their experiences and become the best version of themselves? How can people shift their unfavorable past and current circumstances to a happy and purposeful life? This desire to learn more and help more people motivated me to become a therapist and study spiritual principles with the Dalai Lama.

Spirituality became a major part of my growth and a teaching tool to work with others. Even after thirty years meditation is still part of my daily routine. Through it, I've learned to build trust in myself and others; I've learned to let go of resentment. I forgave my parents and even people who were unforgivable. I became free from my past and began to live a purposeful life.

Your Future Possibility

Author Santosh Kalwar once said, "Trust yourself, you will start to trust others." What if trust was not an issue for you anymore? How would you relate to yourself and others? How would you describe your inner and outer world? What would your relationship with family, friends, and the most intimate partner in your life look like?

This is what I see for you:

- You would be free
- You would feel safe and secure
- You would be happy and satisfied
- You would feel loved and know your love was also received
- You would not blame or judge yourself or others
- You would live in peace and harmony
- You would have an intimate, loving relationship without the fear of losing it.

Mary, a client of mine, came to me to let go of her anger, stress, and anxiety. She had been unmotivated and felt something wrong with her after an unsuccessful business lunch. She knew herself as a powerful, independent woman who handled difficult situations well. However, she was experiencing emotional outbursts with people she loved, like her mother. Mary related to her mother as an anxious complainer, a weak woman she needed to take care of.

That angered her. Mary didn't like how she felt and kept telling me, "I am not myself." I gave her homework to start journaling. We started with a gratitude list then added three things she likes about herself every day. She also started to meditate daily. Mary became aware that she resented her mother's perceived weakness and never wanted to be like her. We built her self-esteem and acceptance of unwanted emotions. Her anger towards her mom and herself slowly subsided. She felt happier and more connected to her mother.

After two months, Mary shared this feedback with me:

> Today I felt proud of myself for not standing up to my mom and telling her she needs to let things go and not be so picky on small things. I did my best to meditate…I accepted that I can't change people and that's okay. Still proud of myself for doing my best because that's really all I can do…I am proud of myself for continuing to trust and express myself.

My life is richer by experiencing my clients' success. This is why I do the work I do.

ABOUT THE AUTHOR: Klara is a professional counselor and certified relationship and success coach who has served the greater Denver community for the past two decades. She is a longtime student of professional development and spiritual principles; her passion developed from various challenges and her healing process to work with divorced professional women. Her coaching accelerates their results and creates a richer and more fulfilling life. Klara provides a customized, highly effective, unique approach that is a combination of therapy and coaching. She lives with her husband in sunny Florida.

Klara Brown
KatalaystforBravery.com
klara@katalystforbravery.com
303-547-4704

CHAPTER 11

#WAKEUPPRAYUPBOSSUP
Margi Ruiz

I *recently lost it with my family. It was an ugly scene that reminded me why I started on this path in the first place. And while I have come a long way, I understand that this is a lifelong journey with no destination.*

"Brothers and sisters, I know that I still have a long way to go. But there is one thing I do: I forget what is in the past and try as hard as I can to reach the goal before me."
~ Philippians 3:13

I remember the day I finally got the nerve to ask my friend Christie what the heck she and her husband did for a living. I had been watching them for some time and was always amazed by how relaxed they seemed and how much time freedom they had. They were always traveling all over the world with their kids, yet managed to be present at all school functions. One day I went on a class fieldtrip and Christie's husband asked me where my husband was. I had to laugh as I said to him, "The day you see my hubby on a field trip, hell has officially frozen over." That's when I gave in to my curiosity.

It was an absolutely beautiful day, so Christie and I decided to go on a walk on the beach. As the waves crashed right next to our feet, I listened intently as she told me all about her life as an entrepreneur and how they had achieved time and financial freedom. Say what??? That's a *thing*? My wheels started turning. What if there was a different way?

See, from the outside we appeared to have it all together. My husband had a great career, we lived in a beautiful home, had four beautiful kids, and attended church regularly. Yes, we were certainly blessed, but things weren't quite as perfect as it seemed. My husband worked all the time and I ran around like a chicken with my head cut off, helping him with his business, chauffeuring the kids around, keeping up with the house, and—worst of all—keeping up with the Joneses. AND we had a dirty little secret. Mental illness was running our home.

My husband of twenty-one years is an absolutely amazing and beautiful man, but he fights some scary demons. Fighting demons is a family affair. I spent all my time hiding it, pretending that things were different, keeping up a facade that everything was perfect. It was exhausting. I felt responsible for his actions and even apologized for things I did not do, wondering if it was somehow my fault. I started letting myself go little by little. I truly have no clue why I was so concerned about what people thought! I have no idea why women, and especially us moms, feel so called to love and serve everyone else but not think about ourselves at all.

My hubby and I met through mutual friends. We had both recently divorced and were the only single people in a group of marrieds, so it's no wonder we ended up together. On our first date he said to me, "You are going to be mine…that is all there is to it." As a single mom working my ass off, the thought of someone else making a decision for me was enticing. He wanted to be with me all the time (it was not a healthy obsession, but when you are in love you are blinded to reality). He made me feel like a prized possession, and he fell in love with my son. Sometimes I joked that he loved him more than me! Five months later we were married and immediately started the proceedings for my husband to adopt him. To this day they have a beautiful relationship.

While my husband was not diagnosed when we married, I knew some things were not right. At very low points in our relationship, I used to look back and wonder why I married him in the first place. That really speaks more about me than him. When you love someone with a mental illness, it is really easy to put all the focus on them and their issues, and avoid looking at your own—and that was the case with me.

I was broken, having grown up in a very dysfunctional family. My mom was married three times and my dad was married twice, but his second relationship was as unhealthy, if not more so, than the first. I knew nothing about boundaries so it is no wonder that we became an entangled, codependent mess. I had spent my entire life running, always busy, always in a hurry for what's next. I graduated early from high school and went to college at sixteen, far from home. I could not wait to get out. I went back for one summer, but after that I lived on my own. I graduated from college early and joined the workforce the week after my twentieth birthday. Busy became my drug. Being successful kept me from looking at and dealing with my depressive thoughts and lack of self-worth. Being an overachiever became my measuring stick.

When Hubby and I first married we had a blast! He treated me like a princess, lavishing me with expensive jewelry and gifts. We traveled all the time, and would have to buy new suitcases to bring home all the stuff we had bought. As a newlywed who had no clue about the finances, this was a fairytale! I remember the day he told me he did not want me to work. I had worked really hard and had a great career in retail. Of course, retail is not just a job, but a lifestyle, with insane hours and working weekends and holidays. He was not into that at all. I remember thinking how ironic it was that just a few months before I was a single parent with no help at all, and here I was being asked (very strongly) to give up my career. Which of course I did, letting myself go a little more.

There were more fancy cars, fancy bags, and, as always, constant busyness. I had no idea at the time that the spending and the hectic pace were just attempts to fill our emotional voids. Those bad habits would start us on a very irresponsible financial path.

The fast life we were living included lots and lots of drinking. I mean, we are Puerto Rican—drinking rum is in our heritage. Being Puerto Rican also comes with lots of passion. Our nights could end up in a crazy loving passion, or a crazy not-so-loving fight. When he drank it was like a game of Russian roulette. He could have a few and be fine, and oh so fun; other times, not so much. Things got much worse when he started taking medication that did NOT mix well with alcohol. I am so proud to say that he has been sober for over eight years now. (The last time he drank was on my fortieth birthday party, and you can imagine how that went for him to make the decision to stop.) Previous to that, however, he was caught up in the vicious cycle, and I let myself go a little more.

When you love someone with a mental illness, and commit to supporting them no matter what, your reality becomes "normal"; walking on eggshells is just a way of life. You either forget or have no clue how life is truly supposed to be. I had made a promise to God that I would make this marriage work, and I believe with all my heart that He, along with our incredible faith and the deep love we have for each other, has kept us together. We are each other's lifeline, and even through the challenges we just know we are meant to be together.

This was what I was dealing with as I walked along the beach with Christie that day. It was also the moment I decided to start my own business, mostly in the hope of finding a better way for me and my family. And WOW, did I ever! Christie introduced me to the world of self-development. I started reading books, then attended events and hired coaches. And you know what I found? Myself and my purpose! I started to envision what I really wanted, but more importantly, I learned that I matter too! That I could not keep taking care of everyone else without taking care of me first, and that mental illness could no longer run my household. Four years into this journey I am happy to say that I feel better than I have felt in years. I am in better shape, physically, emotionally, and mentally. I am dreaming again and making those dreams a reality. And most of all, I love myself again—or maybe for the first time!

It has not been an easy journey. When I started taking care of me, I was met with some resistance. See, my husband and four kids were used to me doing everything, never thinking of myself at all. The price of taking care of everyone but yourself is your inner peace and eventually your soul. I was so worn out and exhausted that on many occasions I woke up with my shoes on because I'd been too exhausted to take them off the night before.

The books I read woke me up to the fact that in order to fix the outer world I had to look within. It was a very scary view. I had to deal with my own demons. This was done with therapy, seminars, and coaching. I also had to pray up and ask for guidance as to what God's plan was for my life, rather than my own. And I bossed up and made the decision to change my life!

Along the way I have learned many lessons, the first being that I had to have compassion, for both my husband and myself. I had to stop being so reactive and taking everything so personally. I have learned that being compassionate does not make you weak. I have learned to forgive faster. This was a hard one for me, because I always felt so wounded, but withholding forgiveness was hurting me so much more than the person I was not forgiving. I would spend weeks dishing out the silent treatment and snarky comments, when all the while what I really wanted was some love. I realized I was the one delaying the process. The most important thing I learned is that I must take care of my body, mind, and soul EVERY SINGLE DAY, first and foremost.

I started with a morning routine. No more jumping out of bed and racing from the second I get up to the time I pass out. Today, that routine includes exercise, hydration, reading or listening to something positive, and affirmations. Most importantly, Hubby and I sit together every morning and do a small devotion—praying, giving thanks, and letting go and letting God. This happens BEFORE I do anything for anyone else. So if my day turns into chaos (as most days do) MY needs have already been taken care of. This puts me in a proactive mode, rather than reactive, and calms my mind so I can handle whatever comes my way.

Now I am passionate to help other women #wakeupprayupbossup so they can start loving themselves again and live the life they not only desire, but deserve! You must love yourself while you love someone with a mental illness. And you know what? By seeing me love myself, my family is learning the value of loving themselves as well. Win-win! I am grateful for this loving, beautiful chaos and the growth I continue to have every day.

Last week I received a call that my dad was very ill. I jumped on a plane the next day and spent a week at the hospital with him. Praise God, he is better. My dad is a big part of the reason I do what I do. He did not take care of his health and is currently paying the price. He told me that if he has one regret, it's not exercising and prioritizing his health. Life is hard; our choice is whether we choose hard now or hard later. Getting up early and making yourself exercise is hard, but it's even harder to have poor mobility when you are old. I did not take care of myself at all while I was with my father at the hospital, and I arrived home emotionally and physically drained.

Sure enough, that first night my teenager was being a teenager and I lost it. I blew up like a bomb, and what should have been a small dispute turned into a massive family explosion. By the next day, which happened to be Mother's Day, it had all blown over, but had I been rested and in a good place physically, emotionally, and spiritually, things probably would not have escalated in the first place. The whole disaster reminded me that taking care of myself first, is not selfish, but selfless. It was just another lesson in the beautiful, purposeful, ever-evolving journey that has become my life.

ABOUT THE AUTHOR: Margi Ruiz is a successful entrepreneur, missionary, coach, and speaker. Originally from Puerto Rico, she now lives in sunny Florida with her hubby of twenty-one years and their four children. She is a graduate of Texas Christian University. After years of hiding the mental health issues in her home, Margi had let herself go completely. Exhausted and numb, she started a journey of self-development that led her to wake up, pray up, and boss up to completely change her life. She is passionate about helping other moms #wakeupprayupbossup as they navigate their families through the chaos of mental health.

Margi Ruiz
margiruiz.com
info@margiruiz.com
facebook.com/margi.gp6
instagram.com/margi.gp6

CHAPTER 12

Navigating the Quicksands of Life

Ashley Gustafson

There are a lot of struggles I could write about when reflecting on my life; however, I no longer look at them as struggles but rather opportunities I have been able to learn and grow from. Was that always my mindset? Absolutely not. I went through the "Why Me?" pity parties; the "I can't do this"; "I'm so alone"; "No one cares"; "Why am I not good enough?"; "It's all my fault"; and so many more blaming and self-doubt scenarios when faced with challenges or consequences of decisions I'd made. In this chapter I will focus on a few situations that impacted my life and how making the choice to believe in myself, become resourceful, lead life from my heart, and have a growth mindset allowed me to pursue my passion for helping others. As a businessowner, inspirational speaker, interactive workshop presenter, fitness creator, and confidence coach, I strive every day to provide people of all ages with the tools they can use to effectively navigate what I call life's personal and professional quicksands.

As a child I was always happy and loved to be adventurous. I was extremely competitive, and on a scale of one to ten my energy was around a hundred. I was very social and always looking to explore, create, enjoy what was around me, and test the waters whenever I could. I also had a very sensitive side and when I was frustrated or anything negative was said to me I took it to the depths of my heart.

Everything changed when I hit my teen years. My parents divorced, and the upheaval led to my living with various friends and boyfriends and their families. I felt like I could do whatever I wanted, and what I wanted was to play soccer—my only healthy outlet—and party with my friends. My grades declined, and I used drugs and alcohol to numb the sadness inside. I loved being around people because I felt like I mattered, but most of them had no idea about the demons that were ripping me apart inside.

During my senior year of high school, I was admitted to the hospital after taking ecstasy—an experience that would change my life forever. Once the doors of the locked unit closed behind me, I had no choice but to look at my own life and deal with myself. Who was I? I was a teenager who felt lost, scared, alone, not good enough, scattered, misunderstood, unloved, and like my whole life had finally fallen apart. I had to make a decision: keep doing what I was doing and end up God knows where, or make changes. I began asking myself, "What do I want in my life?"; "What is important to me?"; "Where do I want to be in the future?"; "Who am I and Who do I want to be?" Answering these questions meant digging deep inside to polish the diamond I had tarnished with my choices and start making decisions that would allow me to create the new life I craved.

Change is a process. The first thing I had to do was forgive myself for the mistakes I had made and figure out how to love me for me. I had to start doing things to better my life, and this meant moving from a fixed mindset to a growth mindset. I attended counseling sessions and became focused on the incremental steps I needed to take to make my visions a reality.

I was accepted into only one college so that decision was easy to make. When I first saw Westfield State College, I thought, *This is a place where I can start over. I can reinvent myself!* I found out very quickly that my minimal efforts in high school now made college courses extremely difficult. Before long I found myself picking up more shifts at work and skipping classes because I didn't think I was smart enough or "good enough." I eventually left Westfield State, moved in with my dad, and enrolled at Quinsigamond Community College to pursue an Associates Degree in General Studies. Imagine my surprise when I walked into a class called "Introduction to the Human Body" and saw that the professor was Mr. Hurley, one of my high school teachers. That day I made another decision that changed my life forever. I decided that I wanted to become a high school teacher so that I could have a positive impact on adolescents, the way Mr. Hurley impacted his students. Though I hadn't given much thought to it back in high school, Mr. Hurley was an incredible teacher. He always took the time to listen, and he was supportive, kind, funny, authentic, and passionate about helping students—not only in the subject he taught but in all aspects of life. He made me want to do whatever it took to become a teacher, and that meant believing in myself. Sure enough, I finished my classes at Quinsigamond and received my Associates Degree in General Studies.

The next semester I attended Worcester State College to pursue a Bachelor's in Secondary Education with a minor in Health Education. To keep my grades up I became a regular at the tutoring center, surrounded myself with people who were passionate about impacting others, and gravitated toward professors who I saw were successful at connecting with their students. Suddenly, I was a straight-A student and excited to complete my projects and assignments. I realized I *was* smart enough, was good enough, and my thinking shifted from "I'll never be able to do this" to "I got this!" I was also working full-time as a bartender and, with some help from supportive people in my life, was able to pay my tuition. On the day of my graduation I felt accomplished, proud, smart, happy, successful, motivated, and determined that I would make a difference in the world by helping adolescents believe in themselves, learn from mistakes, have fun, and embrace learning in all aspects of life.

I applied to be a high school educator for the Dudley-Charlton Regional School District and was hired after just one interview. A girl who had once believed she was not good enough now felt on top of the world! I instantly took what I had learned in my life and applied it to my career, including surrounding myself with mentors and teachers who shared my passion for helping kids and pushed me to be better. For the next twelve years I taught Introductory and Advanced Nutrition; Health; and Physical Education. I also held the roles of Wellness Coordinator, Girls Junior Varsity Soccer Coach, Department Coordinator, Game Change Advisor, SADD Advisor, and Class Advisor. I found the most rewarding part of teaching was not the subject matter, but learning about my students and helping them see their own magnificence while providing them with tools they could use not only in school but throughout their entire lives.

Another significant milestone was becoming independent and able to financially support myself. I had worked very hard to become an educator, but that wasn't enough; I now set a goal to reach the top of the pay scale. While teaching full-time I completed my master's degree, then my "plus sixty credits," which also boosts salary, all while bartending part-time. I felt unstoppable, determined, committed, and so proud of myself. When I stepped back and looked at my accomplishments, I realized that they all stemmed from the changes I'd promised myself I'd make during my hospitalization at UMASS. Simply stated, I chose me, and through that choice I had discovered my purpose: helping others learn from life's quicksands rather than sinking.

Going to college was important, but it was not the defining moment in my life. It was the decision to believe in myself, not quit, go all-in, be resourceful, sacrifice, embrace the difficult, choose mentors who I admired, and put words into action that made the difference. It doesn't matter what you choose, what matters is that it is important to you and that you put everything into it. It all starts with the decision to embrace change instead of resisting it. When we embrace progress and take risks that can improve our lives, that is when our diamond begins to sparkle brighter.

Eventually, I stepped away from teaching to start my inspirational speaking business, Navigating Through Quicksand, LLC. Since then it has expanded to offer personal and professional development, interactive workshops, fitness sessions, and confidence coaching. This has enabled me to help larger audiences and make more of an impact on the world through my experiences and the knowledge gained in all of my roles.

Part of my work is with student athletes, which has become especially important given the impact Covid19 has had on our youth. High school athletics have always had a place in my heart because the soccer team was a refuge after my parents' divorce. The lessons an adolescent learns by being part of a team are countless and priceless. Running athletic fitness sessions is a passion of mine, and I provide these students with tools to help them embrace uncertainty, unite, connect, encourage, and go all-in while decreasing their stress and anxiety. These tools are useful not only while playing their sport, but when dealing with the various quicksands they will encounter in life.

I also continue to devote time to my own growth. I am a firm believer that success leaves clues, and if you want to be your best you should seek out knowledge from those who have been there and done that. Zig Ziglar, Jim Rohn, Tony Robbins, Gabby Bernstein, Mel Robbins, and Oprah, to name a few, took struggle and created a life of fulfillment with it, and they teach the rest of us to do it too. I am always listening to podcasts and attending conferences to improve myself, to keep my diamond shining brightly so that I can help others shine too! Do I have bad days? YES. Do I still doubt myself? YES. Do I fear things? YES. The difference is I don't stay in that place anymore. I have learned, and am still learning, to shift once those feelings come.

I am also a big proponent of nonjudgement and accountability. So often we judge people before we know what they have been through. We tend to point fingers instead of taking responsibility for ourselves. We say things about others like we have never been in a similar situation or overreacted before. We are all human and we are not perfect. The more we come from an open heart and live from a place of compassion and empathy, the more we will realize we are making a difference and building our dreams while encouraging others to pursue theirs as well.

Everyone has a story and those are just a few glimpses of mine. During those challenging times I was also dealing with issues around trust, vulnerability, insecurities, doubts, fears, relationships, and trying to seem like I had it "all together." There are so many areas of life and not all of them will be one hundred percent all of the time. Creating balance is key, and that is why reflecting, being kind to yourself, setting goals, and understanding that there is no such thing as perfect will help you make your visions become your reality. When we take care of ourselves first and become aware of what we would like to improve in our lives, we are that much closer to creating that inner balance and achieving better outcomes in every situation we find ourselves in.

I found my purpose by embracing the struggles and mistakes I'd made, and continue to make. On the rare occasion I struggle with self-doubt, I remind myself that perfection is just an illusion.

The only goal is to be better than I was yesterday, and that is what I continually work toward so I can be a rock that creates a positive ripple effect in the world and provides others with the tools to navigate the quicksands of life.

ABOUT THE AUTHOR: Ashley Gustafson is an Author, Inspirational Speaker, Interactive Workshop Presenter, Fitness Creator and Confidence Coach. She is a woman who follows her heart and lives with passion, creating the life she has always envisioned while helping others do the same. Ashley is the founder and CEO of Navigating Through Quicksand, LLC where she embraces challenges as opportunities to learn, grow, and succeed in all aspects of life. A former high school educator, Ashley holds a master's degree from Worcester State College and her "plus sixty credits" from Augustana University. Currently, she is creating summer fitness camps for high school athletes.

Ashley Gustafson
Navigating Through Quicksand, LLC
Navigatingthroughquicksand.com
Ashley@navigatingthroughquicksand.com
1-800-447-0312

CHAPTER 13

Finding New Purpose After 40

My Social Media Adventure

Francine Sinclair

I had been a stay-at-home mom for thirteen years when I took a good look at my kids and saw how fast they were growing. I realized it would be only a few short years before they were out on their own and I would be left with far too much time on my hands. I was in my early forties and couldn't get a corporate job after so many years out of the workplace—what's more, I really didn't want to. Been there, done that.

After much pondering, I started thinking that starting my own business might be an option. I was homeschooling my kids at that point, and one day while scrolling through Facebook groups for homeschool moms I saw a post by a woman who was doing well selling products on Amazon. I connected with her, and she gave me a lot of information about how she sourced her products and what she did to sell them for a good profit. I also watched a lot of videos, read a lot of articles, and began immediately implementing what I learned. For three years I ran my own e-commerce business on Amazon, with moderate success. However, entrepreneurship can be such a lonely road, and talking to suppliers in China in the middle of the night was not my favorite thing to do. In fact, the only thing I enjoyed about my business was the creative parts and social media marketing. Eventually it occurred to me that maybe I could shift my entire business to social media management for other small business owners. A course or two later, I felt ready to take on the world. I started cold-calling local businesses over the phone and in-person to offer them my services, which many thought was "old-school" and a little bit crazy!

I also had to deal with the insecurity of starting in a new industry. Then someone suggested I get my feet wet by working with a few clients for free. It would turn out to be some of the best advice I've ever received. My first two clients were in completely different fields—one in video production and the other in fashion—which presented a learning curve. I was most familiar with Facebook and Pinterest, while the best platform for these clients was Instagram. Determined to not do anything that looked less than professional, I spent a few days visiting hundreds of profiles and watching dozens of videos. As I looked at the feeds of perfect photos of people with no wrinkles and perfect hair, I had the nagging feeling of not being good enough or knowledgeable enough. Even worse, I felt like I might be too old to be in this business. Though there were many times when I just wanted to drop it all and run, I hung in there and eventually recognized the enormous amount of creativity and wisdom I had to offer my clients to help them achieve their business goals.

My experiment with cold-calling abruptly ended on March 13, 2020, when the world shut down. Suddenly I was back staring at my computer screen, wondering how I was going to connect with people to meet new prospects and get actual paying clients. At first, I took to the phone again and quickly found that many people I needed to speak to were not in their offices and very difficult to reach. Only a few days before I'd been out in my community, shaking people's hands and offering my services like in the old days. Now that community might as well have been on the other side of the planet.

I have to say, I became very discouraged for a week or two. The things going on in the world were weighing heavily on me, and I was too preoccupied with finding toilet paper, masks, disinfectant, and thermometers to focus on my business. At some point, it sunk in that it was going to take more than two weeks to "flatten the curve," and I decided to start focusing on networking online and building those relationships at a much deeper level than I had done previously. It took a while to get used to the back and forth of social media comments and private messages, not to mention the follow-up, but eventually I started to meet clients around the world and see results without leaving my house. I still hope to establish a local client base, but I'm grateful for the opportunity to work with people I wouldn't have otherwise met.

Many of these new contacts were speakers, consultants, and brick-and-mortar business owners who, like me, were suddenly unable to do business as they had before covid. They now had to embrace the "new normal," meaning relying largely on social media. The good news was that this type of entrepreneur usually has a lot of content in the form of videos, articles, and books collected throughout their years—they simply did not have the time or inclination to repurpose it for Facebook, Instagram, and other platforms. I also noticed that the social media connections they did have were not their ideal audience, but mostly friends, family, and random people, so even when they did post about their business no one really cared. Lastly, I could see how there was hardly any engagement on their posts, due to a lack of understanding that social media is a two-way conversation and not a place to just drop your content and run. My biggest challenge was getting people to understand that this engagement with their followers, whether it be on comments or private messages, is the bridge that brings the content and the sales together. Most people want to go directly from posting content to making a sale, but it usually doesn't work that way unless you're doing ads. Organic social media requires nurturing and follow-up that bring leads, sales, collaborations, friendships, and eventually the ability for monetization. A big mistake that I find on Facebook, for example, is that people are using business pages in an attempt to create organic social media content, which unfortunately doesn't happen much at all.

Most of my clients are forty years and older, which is intentional because I so strongly identify with this group. I find that entrepreneurs in that demographic aren't big fans of social media; they generally don't enjoy taking and posting a lot of pictures of themselves, and videos can be a challenge as well. Of course I'm generalizing, but all the things that are required for getting visibility on social media do not come naturally to many of us who grew up before the internet and smart phones. We remember the days when if we wanted pictures of ourselves someone else had to be around to take them. We were also limited to the amount of film in our camera and had to wait to have the photos developed. There were no "retakes," so we really tried our best to look good in every photo; certainly no one wasted an exposure by taking pictures of their coffee or food! Though selfies have been around for quite some time, it still doesn't feel natural to some of these folks. As they say, "Old habits die hard!"

I absolutely love teaching the ins and outs of social media strategy to my clients. Planning what to post and working together to create their content, as well as the strategy that goes along with it, is always exciting. Many of them make things more complicated than they have to be and just need someone to guide them through the process. Some want me to do most of the work for them; some want me to teach them how to do it. My favorites are those who start out highly resistant to the idea of using social media to become more visible. Yes, they want people to notice their business, but they don't want people to notice them. So, though I consider myself a strategist, this is when I put on my coach's hat and help them navigate the platform. It's amazing to see them turn the corner and use social media more confidently to get the results they're looking for.

A tool that has recently gained popularity is social audio, which enables people to do voice marketing without having a podcast. Clubhouse is my favorite platform in this area, and it's been a game-changer both for me and my clients, many of whom don't love video. I feel the same about it. I would agonize for hours over what to say, as well as the lighting, my hair, and my makeup. I even got myself a teleprompter and decided I didn't like it at all. When I discovered this new platform, I realized that I can have quality interactions in real-time with other people. There's something about people hearing your voice and actively listening to you, without the additional distraction of video, that seems really effective in terms of attracting new clients, collaborators, and even friends. You can gather and talk to others, which alleviates loneliness and increases the speed at which you can build a relationship. The challenge with this type of marketing is that you are live; therefore, you have to be very intentional and have a clear-cut strategy; otherwise, you might spend too much time on it (it's addictive!) and not get any results.

I usually advise my solopreneurs to focus on only one social media platform, whichever their audience is on. The exception is Clubhouse, which is linked to either their Instagram or Twitter account, and will require a bit more work. I know all this can be overwhelming, especially when a new platform or app comes out. This is the case with many of my clients—once they feel comfortable with one thing in the digital space, they don't like having to learn another. I get it. I have the same reluctance. I also love helping them embrace change (after all, there's nothing we can do to stop it) and stay ahead of the curve.

I no longer believe that I'm too old for anything (with a few exceptions). We live in challenging times, but the beauty is that we truly have access to learn and do whatever we want. You don't have to pose in a bikini to get attention or be someone that you are not. You can be exactly who you are, and as you increase your visibility the right people will be drawn to you. Still don't believe me? Just give it a try.

ABOUT THE AUTHOR: Francine Sinclair is a social media strategist and the founder of Francine Sinclair Social Media. She focuses on small business owners forty years and older, and helps her clients get, on average, ten times the engagement, visibility, and leads. Francine lives in Tampa, Florida with her husband, son, and daughter, where they enjoy having random pool parties, sometimes with no guests. One of her favorite things to do is spend time at the beach, and she always looks forward to going home to Puerto Rico and hanging out in a place called Piñones, where they sit on the sand, eating fritters and drinking coconut water under the palm trees.

Francine Sinclair
Francine Sinclair Social Media
francinesinclair.com
hello@francinesinclair.com
770-335-4223

CHAPTER 14

Connecting the Dots
Deborah Lynn Strafuss

L iving with purpose is sometimes a question of finding our purpose—connecting the dots and gaining the perspective to perceive the bigger picture.

When I was a child, I delighted in a page full of dots.

Putting my pencil to the paper and moving slowly along, stopping now and then to search for the next dot in the sequence, a beautiful mystery unfolded before my eyes. The dots were not always where I expected them to be. The lines I was drawing curved in, out, and around, sometimes making no sense, but as I followed their course the image became clear.

Similarly, living with purpose does not mean we always know where we are going or who and what we are becoming. We just keep moving, following the dots, and oftentimes the picture does not turn out as we expected.

The power of purposeful living, therefore, lies in the intention to live in awareness rather than realization of the whole picture. Moments of choice are the dots, creating the unique turning points around which the picture pivots and forms. Becoming aware of the power of choice transforms living into creating and allows us to begin to see the picture of our life as it forms. Creating is purposeful; even though it may not know the outcome, it holds an intention to create beauty, an experience, a message, an effect, a result.

My purpose is to find, develop, and express my gifts and talents for the healing of self and others. I have a deep intuitive sense of wellness and health that has followed me all my life. Now that I am approaching seventy, I can look back and see that the dots were clear; however, their pattern was *not* apparent as I wove my way through difficult places, choosing paths to lead me out of confusion into light and peacefulness. The process continues endlessly—the difference is that I work with it consciously now, welcoming the transformative process of healing.

By sharing my story, I am encouraging you to look back through your life and find the dots, connect them, and begin to rejoice in the mystery of creation that is you. We are vast, exciting beings in the process of creating ourselves as we find and connect with who we truly are. This is what Ralph Waldo Emerson meant when he referred to life as "the great experiment." Experiment and experience have the same Latin root, to test or try. The root of this great experiment of life is our experiences; they are the medium through which we create ourselves. We are life artists.

Often healers become so through working with themselves, and I am no exception.

My first conscious dot appeared when I was eighteen and struggling to be myself without feeling suffocated. Beneath the lovely-looking waters of my family were destructive currents threatening to drown me, so I broke the surface and, gasping for air, swam for the nearest—and, as it turned out, very rocky—shore. I cut my feet, hands, and heart in an explosive early marriage to a young Vietnam veteran with at that time unknown, unrecognized PTSD. The lack of healthy family relationships growing up showed itself immediately in my life choices. I remembered my father recounting his WWII experiences and began to realize how wounded he had been. I could not, however, escape my own unconscious imprint as his daughter, and thus had chosen another wounded warrior. Yet, even then, the pencil was moving away from the depths of self-ignorance, toward the light of self-knowledge.

Should you find yourself upon rocky shores, look for imprints from the past that need to be released, and keep scrambling.

The next dot came as an abrupt and unwelcome turn into my healing path. I was six months pregnant, living in my parents' summer cottage on Cape Cod. I had just thrown my drunken, unfaithful young husband out of the house and now shivered alone in the frigid January night.

I listened to the winter winds howl as they tore down my TV antenna, my only connection to the outside world. I was totally alone. I looked back over my short, difficult life, recounting my failures, and gazing on my hopelessness. Here I was floundering on the stormy seas of life again, this time beyond my capacity to navigate. My meager supply of strength was gone. I was used up.

I stared down into the inky blackness of letting go, set to abandon my life. I could not take my body with me because it housed another life; I was, however, ready to let my sanity go. As I stared into the depths of self-destruction, poised to slip beneath the beckoning wave of insanity, the next dot appeared. It was a pause; a split second, a lightening-flash in the darkness of my soul.

And in that one thin moment I made a final appeal to anything in the universe for help. I was on my knees beside the bed, like a good little girl remembering to say her prayers before going to sleep.

Something strange—I describe it as a "whoosh"—went right through me. As it did, all my intense overwhelming emotions of fear, anger, hopelessness, and despair vanished. The huge storm that had raged just seconds before was replaced by a sudden and complete calm.

I picked up my head from the side of the bed and peered down the length of the living room from my open door. There was a white form walking away from me down the room. I only saw its back. It did not turn around. It reached the end of the living room and turned into the kitchen and was gone. So was my despair.

The story does not end there, although that was a miraculous incident and a wonderful gift. I had gotten a taste of peace and clarity; now it was up to me to make it mine to keep. That turned out to mean working through many places needing healing in my life. One miracle does not make a life; it begins a transformation. Big dot. In the subsequent years, I was the proverbial onion, patiently (and sometimes not so patiently) peeling off and healing each layer of my life, and then the next, and the next after that.

I was a wounded healer. All my child's life I'd tried to lighten the burden of the pain and sorrow of my parents' broken relationship, broken dreams, and broken lives by taking them on myself. The healer in me did not know any other way. A child ingesting adult pain is severely and deeply impacted. Now I had fatherless children of my own to rear, and filling them with something other than pain was my immediate life purpose and goal. It was a huge investment in my own healing to offer them hope and love as I learned and grew.

For me, that meant working with wise and spiritual counselors. I learned to work and live with others in an active community with healthier structures than those with which I had grown up; I learned to release anger, hurt, shame, and guilt by emptying the reservoirs of pain I had unknowingly accumulated. I built muscles of trust and faith by choosing to believe in love and light. I learned to hope steadfastly for the best and did the personal work spirit revealed as needing healing, such as learning to communicate in healthy ways, learning to parent differently, learning to pray, and learning that all prayer is answered even through dark and difficult times when things appear to be getting worse. This is hard work. It takes dedication and motivation. Fortunately, my drive for sustained personal sanity and opening to experience the joy of living was so strong I could not give up. The only other option was to live the deadened life I nearly chose that lonely night on Cape Cod.

Looking back, I see this as the path of the healer. It is fueled by a vision, by an intuitive knowledge of the best there is available in human existence and a clear choice to pursue that vision actively and fully. We all carry the seed of this vision of life. We are born with it.

I was not aware of these universal truths at the time they were happening. I only saw my struggling self, trying not to drown in self-pity. The beauty of looking back and connecting the dots comes with time. It comes with a soul that is humbled and awed by the capacity of humanity to heal itself. It comes with learning to look backward and forward patiently and unflinchingly, anchored to one's truth in the present. These are spiritual skills for living that all of us have the capacity to cultivate and grow—usually with a little help from our friends, advisors, and the wise ones to whom we turn. Life is not a solo journey. Living is not an isolated experience.

After seven years of self-healing work, I met and married my second husband—who was also a veteran blessed with PTSD—and had three more children. Lots more dots. Deeper levels of healing were needed as we walked through his issues, which raised more of mine along the way. Together we stumbled through the paths of healing to bring hope and change to family patterns of alcoholism and depression; finally recognizing and healing the roots of PTSD; and releasing karmic curses carried through generations. We worked to heal relationships and create clearer paths for our children to grow in. We created a deeper, richer partnership to live in. Now we offer healing to others through counseling, coaching, Reiki, and spiritual healing. Our personal healing continues.

Intentional choices, healing choices, become clear as our inner muck is flushed out and we awaken, often with help from others. Our conscious intentions activate purpose and change the course of life. Following the Reiki precepts[1] for living a happy life allows us to release fear, anger, and worry and grab hold of gratitude and

---

1   https:// ihreiki.com/reiki_info/five_elements_of_reiki/reiki_precepts

compassion as we become aware of our choices and find the spiritual energy to stay on our healing course.

I share these dots, these life challenges and turning points, to encourage, strengthen, and support others wrestling through the pains and burdens of living. For those mired in disappointment, self-loathing, trauma, and despair. For the hopeless, the wounded. For the cross-wired, the addicted, the afflicted. A cure may not always be achieved in this lifetime, but we have access to the ongoing process of healing which prepares the life for its continued journey, here and beyond, by strengthening the soul and freeing the spirit.

Today I see the web of family life being slowly restored and healed. PTSD, drug addiction, alcohol addiction, depression, suicide, and emotional pain are healing one thread, one life, at a time, stretching out from that original choice, fueled by continuing attention and intention. As each strand is lightened and rewoven into the tapestry of life it affects every other strand. It heals both past and future, as all are interconnected and woven together. The pattern of your dots, combined with my own and those of all other souls, creates a larger and more beautiful design than any of us can imagine. On an individual level, this reweaving brings joy and abundance; on a family level it brings generational healing; and on a global level it brings light and restores balance to the planet.

Should your mind balk at understanding this web of connection, consider the invisible yet understandable worldwide web humans have created using kinetic energy via a network of devices. We recreate what we intrinsically know and are. Woven together in our energetic fields of influence and confluence, we and all others are the sentient devices comprising the web of life that flows with the shared energy of source. Each connection matters and counts and each faulty, weak connection impairs the whole. Each restored strand links to every other strand, strengthening the light and healing the whole.

Set a course with whatever intention you hold. Like a seed, no matter how small, a tiny dot in the jumble of life, stake an intentional point for growth, for recreating and moving forward with purpose. This can be done right now, right here. Pause and state the intention that has been growing in your heart. Speak it into the world with your breath. Write it in your journal. Paste it on your wall. The beauty of your design will become clear as you twist, tack and turn following the thread of your intention through each life experience. This is purposeful living, and you are the master artist of your life. One gift, one life, always re-workable; the planet is waiting for your unique creation, your purposeful expression.

ABOUT THE AUTHOR: Deborah Lynn Strafuss is a Reiki Master Practitioner and Teacher, a Spiritual Life Coach, Shamanic Practitioner, author, and poet. She opened Crystal Reiki in 2012 after learning Reiki to cope with the challenges of her mother's Alzheimer's Disease. A mother of five and grandmother of twelve, Deborah is also a Sacred Childbirth with Reiki™ practitioner working with birth and rebirth. She brings her focus to life transitions using healing modalities to assist her clients in transforming life experiences into spiritual strengths for living with grace, beauty, strength, and purpose. Find her poetry at DeborahLynnBeginnings.com and her cathartic healing Alzheimer's story at On-Angels-Wings.net.

Deborah Lynn Strafuss, RMT, CSLC, SCR™,CDP
CrystalReikiEnergy.com
HealingHands@CrystalReikiEnergy.com
508-353-5136

CHAPTER 15

Look Within for Purpose, Power, and Peace

Mousami Pandey

I used to live life in a black and white fashion. I believed there was a "right" way to live, which was go to a good school, get good grades, get a nice job, make good money, get married to the love of your life, and be happily ever after. Not to toot my own horn, but I believed I had it all. I came to the US for my undergrad degree and went on to complete my graduate degree. I got married to my high school sweetheart, we purchased our first home together, and adopted a six-month-old rescue puppy. I worked hard for years building an investment practice for my employers and eventually was managing a half-billion dollars in investment portfolios. Then, after working hard for years and checking off everything on my list, came the plot twist of my life: the realization that I was NOT happy.

It took me quite a while to face this because it went against everything I had known to be true. Of course, there were moments of self-reckoning prior to this big conscious realization. The inner knowing that I wasn't happy had been in fact lingering in my consciousness for quite some time. It would pop in once in a while to let me know of its existence, but my ego was too self-righteous, defensive, and deeply entrenched in its identity to admit it. It kept shoving the knowing aside because it did not want anything to threaten the reality it had worked hard to build over the years—not to mention the feelings of guilt, shame, and regrets that came with the thought of losing it. I simply chose to believe that life is not supposed to be easy anyway, and so I took this discomfort as normal and continued to ignore my internal alarm system.

The Universe, however, had other plans for me. My work landscape unexpectedly started changing, which shook me to my core. Suddenly, there was no more hiding or avoiding, and the illusion of identity and station in life that my ego had been so desperate to hold on to started to dissolve.

One day at work, a small incident opened the lid to all the emotions I had been suppressing. I felt deeply sad, heartbroken, and perplexed, and I simply couldn't control the tears. This was extremely strange and embarrassing because I never cry in front of people, let alone my coworkers or bosses. As my emotions came gushing to the surface, I remember thinking, *What is wrong with me?!* It was as if my body was doing its absolute best to tell me, very loudly, that I was out of alignment, that it was high time to pause and reevaluate my career and my life.

As if this wake-up call wasn't enough, more things transpired that left me feeling even more lost, confused, miserable, and disempowered. I started looking past the trivialities of daily life and questioning the meaning of life and what my purpose really was. Unfortunately, I only had questions but no answers. The only thing that became clear for me in that process was that my job was not my path anymore and I had no more reason to pour myself into it. My inner voice said loud and clear, "This is not what you are supposed to do with your life," and this time I decided to honor it. I wasn't exactly sure what I was going to do, but I chose to trust myself and take a leap of faith into the unknown.

I took time off to relax, untie the knots that had taken hold in my heart, and figure things out for myself. I wanted to "just be" without the constant compulsion to be doing something. This was a radical departure for me, but I slowly learnt to enjoy being in the moment without the overhang of to-do lists and other mental noise that I used to carry around constantly.

That August, one of my friends invited me to join her at a ten-day Vipassana meditation retreat in suburban Massachusetts. I instantly jumped at the chance because I had been trying really hard to meditate the last few months, without much success. I immediately went online to sign up for fall session, only to learn there was a wait list. My disappointment turned to excitement when a week before the retreat I received an email saying a spot had opened up! My friend couldn't go anymore because of work, but that did not stop me. I did some research and learned it was a silent meditation retreat, completely free, and run by volunteers. Participants got two meals a day, along with accommodation, and meditated ten to eleven hours a day. The reviews I found online, along with feedback from a friend who had been to this retreat, were extraordinarily positive. All of this gave me confidence that there was nothing to worry about. After educating my husband as to my findings and getting him fully onboard, I confirmed my spot and packed my bags for ten days of noble silence and meditation.

For the first three days of the retreat, we were asked to simply focus on our breathing. As simple as it may sound, any meditation practitioner knows that's not the case. In order to do this well, we've got to first learn to observe the thoughts in our heads without getting caught up by them. We also must realize that when we do get sidetracked (as everyone does) beating ourselves up about it doesn't help the cause. Through the "simple" act of focusing on our breathing, on the touch of breath on our skin, moving in and moving out, we learn to sit still with our thoughts, be okay with our state of mind as it is, and start deepening our concentration.

I really struggled the first two days there. In my determination to meditate well, I was breathing too forcefully and my body hurt all over from sitting cross-legged for hours! It took a lot of patience and continued practice, but eventually I could feel my concentration deepening layer by layer. By the end of the second day, I started feeling certain vibrations around my nose, which I learned, was part of the meditation process. S. N. Goenka, the late Vipassana teacher who helped bring this twenty-five-hundred-year-old meditation technique (passed down by Gautam Buddha) into the global arena, describes these sensations as biochemical and electromagnetic reactions happening throughout our bodies at all times. We are just not usually quiet or focused enough to notice them in our daily lives.

By the sixth day, I was able to feel these subtle body sensations all over my body. Some were subtle, while others were intense. We were taught to refrain from labeling any sensation as good or bad—not an easy task! Sitting cross-legged for hours was also intense, but accepting it for what it is and not reacting with resentment revealed greater insights in return. During one of our meditation sittings, I kept my focus on my throbbing feet for a while and soon noticed that the intense sensations became subtler and subtler. I no longer found it painful, but was able to move past the surface level to observe subtler sensations that were underneath. It was amazing! All I had to do was remain calm, observant, and objective rather than get consumed by pain, agitation, resentment, and repulsion. This made me truly realize that the labels we attach to things, situations, and experiences in life are primarily just our conditioning, and if we can look through it with an open and curious mind we can gain our own unique perspective on things.

I understand that the insights I received were not extraordinary by any means; in fact, most of us already have this knowledge at a conceptual level. To receive it experientially, however, as I did at the retreat, was a game-changer. I think of it as knowledge churning into embodied wisdom. I believe they got ingrained in me from the inside out.

One great accomplishment for me at this retreat was developing the ability to see things from a place of neutrality, without any bias or judgment. This helped me put many of my life experiences into perspective, including my experience at my old job and my strung-up emotions around it. To put it simply, I was finally able to see that I had put my job on a pedestal. In exchange for my time, hard work, dedication, loyalty, and discomfort I had felt all those years, I expected it to fulfill all of my conscious and unconscious needs, desires, and aspirations. And when reality hit that I had actually been living a delusion, it was too much and too sudden to comprehend and left me feeling lost and confused.

Untying this major knot in my heart—and many others in the days that followed—gave me a sense of inner peace and tranquility that I had never before experienced. I felt so calm and astoundingly content, it was magical! And knowing that there is a way to access this peace within made me feel like I had finally found the pot of gold under the rainbow! I decided to savor those moments forever and use them as an inner compass going forward.

My most profound experience, however, came for me on the tenth day of the retreat, when we practiced metta meditation. Metta is a pali word which means "loving kindness." In this meditation we were guided to feel love, warmth, care, and pray for the well-being of all beings—starting with the ones closest to our heart and working our way out to our friends, community, and, ultimately, the world. As I visualized my mom and my family in my mind, I started feeling this sweet and intense feeling of love that swelled my heart and started buzzing through my chest. I thought of my husband and everything he represents for me, and sent him my love. I then thought of my friends and sent them my love as well. As I kept expanding my mind and my heart with my thoughts and feelings of love, I started feeling stronger and stronger loving sensations all over my body. Slowly and gradually—I'm not sure how long this took—I found myself completely engulfed with love, not just within my body but all around me. It felt like I was sitting in a big bubble of it, which was mind-blowing and perplexing at the same time. Tears started rolling down my cheeks and I thought to myself, *We are pure love in our core essence! It is true! I can actually feel it! I know it! It really is true!* I'm not sure how long this experience lasted, but every cell in my body felt drunk on the emotion of love. As the tears continued to roll, I was ecstatic and smiling ear to ear. I then had a realization I would want to share this with everyone I knew: our thoughts and beliefs keep us captive in a cycle of pain, anger, frustration, dissatisfaction, pride, honor, but that it's all just an illusion. Once we see through the illusion, we find there is love, and only love, in our core; that is actually who we really are. I also thought how wonderful it would be if everyone could experience this, realize this, and embody this truth as they go through life.

I couldn't have asked for a better experience to close out the retreat. It completely shifted my outlook on life; it was the moment I decided that love and inner peace would guide me moving forward. In the coming months I would make some major changes—primarily with regard to my career aspirations. I began designing a lifestyle in which I had space to honor my inner work and use my learnings to guide others to honor theirs. I love coaching my clients to cut through the illusions of the mind to find their purpose, true power, and inner peace, and witnessing their growth and transformation is a constant reminder that I am finally walking the path that is meant for me. I highly recommend that everyone out there pause, meditate, and look within often to make sure they are in alignment with their purpose and living life on their own terms. If you need guidance, there are plenty of amazing resources available. Reach out and get the support you need. More importantly, stay open, stay curious, and lead your life with love, and all will be fine.

ABOUT THE AUTHOR: Mousami Pandey is a Certified Purpose Clarity Coach, aspiring motivational speaker, and the founder of A Look Within LLC. Originally from Nepal, she moved to the US with hopes of a brighter future. She holds an MBA and almost a decade of experience in the wealth management industry. An existential crisis led her to make some big changes in her life and, eventually, discover her passion for coaching. Her mission is to guide women who feel unfulfilled and unaligned in their career path to drop all their "shoulds," fully embrace their desires, and live an empowered life of heart-aligned purpose, power, and peace.

Mousami Pandey
A Look Within LLC
alookwithin.net
contact@alookwithin.net
Instagram: @a.look.within

CHAPTER 16

Finding Purpose in Connectedness

Karen Flaherty

It's often said that we're all connected, that though we each have a different life purpose, different energy, and different life paths, we're all just floating as drops in the same ocean of possibility. This is what we say in Human Design, and lots of new people have been jumping on that bandwagon of connectedness lately. For some, it may be the fashionable thing; others may still not believe it or have not given it much thought at all.

So what if we are all connected? Like the root system of the trees or the stars in the sky? What would that mean for you—and for me? How might that change the way we talk to each other? Treat each other, laugh and cry with each other, vote for each other?

In the United States—and in the U.K. and elsewhere—our discourse with each other and via all media has been filled with ideas and the reality of separation for a while now. No one can seem to agree on points of view or even on the facts that those points of view are based on.

What if we went looking for places where that connection happens, and focus on that? We all know that what we focus on amplifies, so why not focus on connectedness rather than separation? Love rather than differences? Compassion rather than who's right in the moment?

We say we're in search of those things. That's what I say, anyway, and that's what most of my clients say too. But our focus has said otherwise. What if we could focus on connectedness just a little more each day, until we reach the magical fifty-one percent mark (more than half is all we need). What would that look like?

I was still wondering this as I dove into a new endeavor with arms open wide and knowing that I couldn't NOT join the group I'd heard about...

"Please answer the question, 'Why am I here?'" the leader of the Zoom call asked sweetly.

On that day in September 2020, I and the other new members of the group were asked that question as a way of introducing ourselves. Actually, it kind of felt like a hazing. Friendly, but still pointed. As if I should account for my attendance in a way that indicated more than just passing interest. It felt more like, "You say you want to be here, but are you committed? Are you one of us? Will you take a stand with us?" Friendly, but serious.

And, as I answered the question—saying something about my interest in social justice—I could feel myself tense up. Here was a group of women I knew and yet I was walking on new ground. Would I say the right thing? They had already been meeting for a few months—since June—and I had never tackled this topic before. Did I have anything to add? Would I just be an onlooker or would I at some point be able to contribute something meaningful?

I wasn't feeling very hopeful at that moment, but I knew I didn't want to stand on the sidelines anymore. It seemed to be late in the game, but I was feeling the pain of seeing Black men and women suffering and dying for reasons that could no longer be tolerated by white people. And once the pain was there, I couldn't go back.

Very few people make a change in their lives until we feel the pain and can't stand it anymore. That's where I was.

The only way forward was to join in somehow. I'm not a marcher (bad knees) and didn't see myself in that role. But I knew I had to do something, and this group seemed like a natural fit at the right time.

As Saint Francis de Sales (1567-1622) said, "Bloom where you're planted."

For the past five years I'd been a member of "University Women of Flagler" –a group of about one hundred members who meet monthly and create fundraisers as a way to finance college scholarships for local female high school seniors. During that I time I had happily taken on various roles, met many lovely women, and am currently part of the Board, serving as editor of the monthly newsletter. A lot of our usual activities around fundraising for scholarships had been curtailed during COVID over the past year, with monthly general meetings and Board meetings happening on Zoom.

There was also the creation of a new discussion group called "Seeking Insights for Solutions" (SIS). Following George Floyd's death on May 25, 2020, one UWF member, Trish, called another, Gina, to wish her a happy birthday and to see how she was doing with the news. What began as a chat between friends quickly turned to a passionate discussion about racial inequality.

Trish is white and Gina is Black.

They decided that if there was ever a time to include others in this conversation, it was now. They invited two other members to their next discussion, and by the time UWF had their Annual Planning Meeting on June 17, the die had been cast. There were four Founding Members—two white and two Black—plus a few other women, and the idea was to continue both the discussion and the make-up of the group so that Black and white women would be equally represented. Would the Board approve a new discussion group within the UWF framework to discuss social justice? Let's just say that at first it was not received with open arms. It was given a provisional "okay and let's see what happens over the summer."

The plan was for the group to discuss topics of the day, the first of which was social justice. I had other commitments over the summer, including a speaking gig at a conference in early September, so I joined later that month. By January, there were thirty members—fifteen Black and fifteen white. This was new for me, for though I had worked in New York and travelled the country, I'd never been to a meeting with more than a few Black people, let alone evenly split. Finally, I felt I would be in meaningful conversations with Black women and hear their perspectives on all that's going on in the country.

After a few discussions over the summer about how to move forward, the group had started doing a lot of research, and conducting cross-racial interviews—with questions suggested by Gina. She worked with another professor to use similar questions in a class they'd taught together years earlier. The survey was kept simple. There were only four questions: all about our histories, how we grew up, what racial interactions we'd had, and what influenced our own opinions about race.

Each pair of women (one white, one Black) would interview each other and then report back at a meeting what they'd found out; they would also describe their partner's history and answers to the questions. The stories were warmly told, with understanding and heartfelt camaraderie that had a very touching effect on all who listened. Overall, the biographies have been very illuminating.

As Gina had hoped, each woman got to tell her own story, from her own perspective to a willing listener/scribe. Then, each woman told her partner's story to the entire group in a way that honored, cherished, and lifted up that life. For many of the women, including me, it was the first time anyone had ever asked. And it was the first time anyone seemed to care. It was revelatory for each of us. As we told our stories, each member got to understand why we think as we do because of the lives we'd lived. Gina's premise—that we would understand each other so much better and from a different perspective if we knew our stories—seemed to be working!

We soon came to realize that these were more than interesting personal anecdotes. All the members happened to be between the ages of fifty-five to eighty years old, so their stories were actually the history of the United States, from before the Civil Rights Movement to the present day. These women were also representative, not only of many different states but other countries as well!

While we found so many contrasts—urban vs. rural settings, private vs. public schools, poverty vs. ample food and housing—we also found so many similarities. Most of us had parents who valued education and knew that education was the way up and out of our circumstances, as well as loving families and supportive schools, teachers, and communities. The friendships that were begun during these shared stories have illustrated just how intimately appreciated each was, in large part because we lived during the same historical period but with opposite perspectives, each looking into a fishbowl from outside.

As we said in our eventual presentation, "Although we realize that systemic racism still exists, the uniqueness of our voices is that we can remember...

A time before the enactment of public policies that brought about change:

- Brown vs. Board of Education (1954)
- Civil rights movements (1950s-1960s)
- Affirmative Action (1964)
- Medicare Act (1965)
- Voting Rights Act (1965)
- Fair Housing Act (1968)
- Public Health & Welfare (1968)

Despite these changes, we have stories that tell the tales of systemic racism."

And, I would add, how we succeeded.

By October, it was obvious to the entire group that what we were discovering and uncovering were gems of history that we wanted to share with others. Some even thought of it as a legacy project, full of ideas and experiences that our children and grandchildren might benefit from hearing.

We decided to create a video about our findings—both cultural and academic. The research being done—in the arenas of healthcare, economics, housing, criminal justice, and education—was just as potent as the stories. I was honored to be part of the Presentation and Production Committees (and became the Technical Director for production and video editing). We came up with a format, created a script from all the stories, taught four of our members to "act" on Zoom with the script as vignettes, created a PowerPoint with all the research, added music from our talented pianist, credits, beginning and ending statements and voila!—we had a thirty-three-minute video presentation. We debuted it to our UWF General meeting in February to almost a hundred Zoom participants and received rave reviews.

We explained the process to our audience this way:

"We invite you to listen to four of our members as they re-tell excerpts from LIVED EXPERIENCES as shared by twenty-five women in our SIS Group during one-on-one interviews.

Four of our members will retell excerpts from the LIVED EX-PERIENCES that represent ALL of the members. The anecdotes they share with you were extracted from twenty-five one-on-one, cross-racial interviews. As a result, our four 'actors' each take on multiple roles."

Gina's goal was to transcend our boundaries and collectively change our community, as she explained to me. As a group, we feel like we're on the way to achieving that goal. And we're so proud of the results. Following the February presentation, many local and national groups have asked to view the video, used it in their church meetings, book clubs, town councils, and other organizations. We created a list of questions to start conversations about race and equality once the video has been viewed in a group.

We are so pleased with the attention and the results, but I must admit that there were times when I felt like giving up. I was dog-tired some weekends from editing and re-editing, making all the changes the group requested, retaping segments over and over again, and moving things around. Did I mention that many in the group are perfectionists, including me, unfortunately? But I kept going.

It felt like a purpose had arisen in my life that I didn't know was there. I didn't know it was coming, and I certainly wasn't looking for it. But once it was there, I couldn't say "no" and I couldn't give it up. I knew it was bigger than me. And I owed it to all the women and men who had fought so hard to get where they are now.

ABOUT THE AUTHOR: Karen Flaherty is a certified Human Design Specialist and the best-selling author of *Getting to Know YOU*. Before finding Human Design in 2009, Karen spent thirty years in marketing, training, and sales positions in New York and New Jersey. She brings this wealth of knowledge of the corporate world, and her own life experience to her Human Design coaching practice. Karen is passionate about helping her clients discover their purpose and their genius. She works with individuals, couples, and families, as well as businesses and entrepreneurs, to find a new way of reinventing their lives in the twenty-first century.

Karen Flaherty
LivingbyHumanDesign.com
amazon.com/author/karenflaherty
youtube.com/c/LivingbyHumanDesign
Social Justice video: youtu.be/DPmJMbEc5iw

CHAPTER 17

My Journey from Despair to Triumph

Angela Hanna

I remember a time when it felt like a dark cloud had engulfed our planet. Life as we knew it was about to change.

January 2020 began with a sudden loss. Our eighteen-year-old cat, the last of three beloved cats we owned, was having trouble with one of her eyes. We were treating it with a prescription from the vet. One morning her eye just did not look right and we had to bring her into emergency. While there, her eye literally liquified. Because she was so senior, the decision to put her down had to be made right there on the spot.

I stood completely helpless and broken in the corner of the vet's office, facing the wall and sobbing. I could not believe that in just a few minutes she would be gone. It was more than I could bear. My heart and spirit were shattered. I returned home that day with nothing but memories and a lock of her velvety soft creamy white hair.

It was the beginning of a year that would nearly break me.

My older son took ill a week later, after traveling to attend a wedding. We thought he had the flu, with a high fever, chills, and chest congestion. He was making progress but it was slow. A few days later I too became sick and of course I believed I had also caught the flu.

The chills were uncontrollable, I could not stop shaking and I was having difficulty taking a full breath. I had never in my life had a flu this severe. There was one night when my entire body was in excruciating pain and I thought I may not wake.

At the time my husband was selling oxygen concentrators for home use.

Luckily we had two remaining units, and I unpacked one of them, hooked it up, and immediately began using it. It offered some benefit but as much as I tried, I could not get the oxygen deep enough into my lungs. I experimented with some movements until I finally found one. I was close to tears when I felt a cool flow of oxygen down deep in both lungs. It took every ounce of my energy to continue this movement a few more times, but it was worth it. I stayed hooked up for many hours a day, and though I began to feel a little better I was nowhere close to normal.

A few days later, my husband and younger son also became ill, but it passed relatively quickly for them. My older son and I took longer to recuperate. The fatigue was overwhelming and would take until the end of May to subside.

A week and a half after having the "flu," I went back to work full-time. I had a persistent cough that was often accompanied by a sore throat. I Skype with clients from all over the world all day long and the constant talking did not help the healing process. It was all I could do after sessions to go lie down and rest. I was feeling completely depleted.

Not long after we got sick, the news of a pandemic was broadcast. The city I live in was deemed a "hotspot" and by March there was a complete lockdown. It was frightening to watch the devastation of families all over the world. People were instructed to leave jobs and schools and quarantine in the safety of their homes.

I however did not have the opportunity to stop or slow down. Even as the majority of people reduced their work hours, mine doubled and on some days tripled.

I am Certified in The Body Code Modality, a form of energy healing. This has been my full-time job for nine years and I love it, but now my phone did not stop ringing. Clients kept coming, and being the compassionate person I am, I could not turn them away. Though my fear, apprehension, anxiety, and sheer terror matched theirs, I had to keep it all together. I had to be strong. These were very difficult times and I was being called to help.

My clients who are nurses would text me in the middle of the night, desperate for a word of comfort. Because I am very empathic, I would feel their pain and when I was done calming them, it would be difficult to contain my own grief.

For the next several months I worked ten- to twelve-hour days. In the fifteen-minute breaks between sessions, I ate whatever I could grab to give me some sustenance and the energy to get through my next session.

It wasn't until Christmastime that I finally got some respite from the grueling schedule, and by early 2021, my practice was slowly returning to a more comfortable and manageable pace.

One morning, as I walked out of the shower I caught a glimpse of myself in the mirror and no longer recognized the woman looking back at me. I had gained a substantial amount of weight. My guess would be at least twenty pounds, though truth be told, I was afraid to weigh myself.

My legs, knees, and ankles were constantly in pain. My back, joints, and bones were in terrible condition. Even if I wanted to integrate a form of exercise into my life, my body was just not going to cooperate. Sitting all day had compressed some discs in my spine and I experienced the debilitating effects of sciatica.

Electrical impulses traveled through my legs and caused me great discomfort. One night I sat in bed and spoke out loud to my legs, "I am so grateful that you have carried me for almost sixty years now, I promise you that from this day forward I will support you as you have supported me." I did not know how I would begin helping myself, but I know that if we are sincere in our intention, whether through meditation or prayer, a solution always appears. The weight gain was not just because of covid—I had been gaining over the last nine years. Perimenopause and menopause made losing it difficult, and despite hours at the gym and dieting for months, the results had been minimal.

Now, my once little "menopause belly" had ballooned and the slender waist I had as a young woman were now covered up by a spare tire of fat. I knew this would not be an easy feat but I could not allow my discouragement to dampen the compassion I now felt for myself. I prayed for help.

I have always been a big believer in a holistic approach to every ailment, and regularly worked on myself energetically, In this case, however, it was not an energetic issue but a mechanical one. The continuous sitting for long periods of time had adversely affected every part of my body, and the extra weight I was carrying compounded the problem and added insult to injury.

I decided I needed to implement a two-fold approach. The first was to strengthen my frame in order to support my body mass, and the second would be to find a way to lose the excess weight.

Collagen kept coming up in my online searches. I found that it had a lot of the benefits that I was searching for. To my surprise, I found out that we are made of ninety percent collagen; it is the glue that holds every organ, gland, and system in our body together. I also learned that collagen is the major component of bone mass.

Other possible benefits of taking collagen were improved joint mobility and less overall discomfort, healthier cartilage and connective tissue, and healthier skin, hair, nails, eyes, and gums. Why had I not heard of this before? It sounded perfect!

I went out and purchased reputable powdered collagen from my grocery store and took it religiously for two weeks as directed, but I was still in pain. I remained hopeful, but when another week passed without relief I was starting to be discouraged.

Later that week, I was speaking to my friend Rachelle in Prince George, B.C. and mentioned how I felt. She asked if I had tried liquid collagen. There was that word again! It seemed everyone knew about it but me.

I told her I had tried the powdered form and had not seen a difference.

She explained that just fifteen to thirty percent of powdered collagen is absorbed, whereas ninety-three percent of the liquid is absorbed, beginning the second we place it in our mouth.

I asked her how she knew so much about collagen and she told me she had partnered with a company and was now selling this award-winning product.

I then shared with her my struggle with weight gain over the last year and how it was affecting my body, mind, and spirit. She told me that this same company had a weight loss system that was voted the number one in the world in 2020. Rachelle added me to a platform so I could witness the real results people were getting.

I took a couple of days to think about whether to give these products a try.

What if they were just gimmicks?

I couldn't deny the many people who posted pictures daily of their incredible weight loss results. The testimonials kept coming, so I cautiously decided to follow my intuition and ordered the products.

In my own energy practice I have worked with a fair amount of clients on emotional eating, self-judgment, negative body image, self-sabotage, and many other emotional blocks that could trigger their overeating and eventual weight gain. Some clients went on to lose weight and some did not. As a matter of fact, some packed on more pounds while they were trying to lose weight.

I realized now that not all weight gain is rooted in emotion. Sometimes it has to do with hormonal imbalances, especially during menopause and after childbirth. Some have to do with the number of toxins we are storing in our bodies.

I learned that toxins are stored in our fat cells. When we "diet" our fat cells begin detoxifying, and our bodies go into a protective state and produce even more fat cells to store the toxins. That made perfect sense to me.

So then, how was this system going to be any different from the others?

It turns out that the ingredients in the product are a first-in-the-world combination of two leading technologies that actually have the ability to shrink fat cells and produce a reduction in fat mass.

I became excited about the possibility of regaining a more youthful body composition. The day I received my products I took a deep breath and took my first spoonful. Despite being optimistic, I was cautious not to get my hopes up too high in case I was one of those people it did not work for.

I began exercising three times a week to expedite any possible weight loss. After the first week, I was in complete disbelief when the scale showed I was three pounds lighter. There must be something wrong with the scale, I thought.

The following week, there was another three pounds off. Fast forward two months and I had lost a total of twenty-four pounds. Clothes that I had not been able to wear now were fitting comfortably. My belly was gone. The roll I had packed on during quarantine was no longer. Going up a flight of stairs was a breeze. No more discomfort, anywhere!

I am proud to say that I will be turning sixty in a few months and I have never felt better. I have more energy and stamina than I did when I was forty. I am now running on the treadmill pain-free and filled with gratitude for the second wind these products provide me with every day.

I am continuing my journey to radiant health and wellness. My experience has been so profound on more than a physical level. There is a sense of confidence and peace that comes over me when I know I am being truly good to myself by giving my body what it needs.

I have since tried many other products from this company and have absolutely loved them all. As a matter of fact, I love and respect its dedication to clean living and overall excellence so much that I have also partnered with them.

I would say that I now offer the best of both worlds, because not only do I help my clients on an energetic level, I also help them achieve their physical health and wellness goals.

My purpose has always been about service to others. Now I feel blessed and grateful for the struggles I endured, as they have paved the road for me to fulfill that purpose on an even deeper level.

ABOUT THE AUTHOR: Angela has been an Empathic Energy Healer for nine years, using primarily the Emotion Code and Body Code modalities to help free clients all over the world of their emotional and physical limitations. After a surge in demand for her services during the 2020 lockdown left her in physical pain, overweight, and exhausted, she prayed for guidance. Not long after, a friend told her about state-of-the-art products that helped her regain control over her health and wellness. Her results were so substantial that Angela has now partnered with this company to help others achieve their best possible health goals. This is a success story, and one she is truly passionate about.

Angela Hanna - Integrated Energy Wellness
integratedenergywellness.com
modere.com/7978712
modere.ca/7978712
angelahanna@hotmail.com ~ 514-894-2351

CHAPTER 18

I Always Have a Choice
Sheila Dunn

Confusion, Fear, and Sadness

As I approached the building someone walking toward me said, "It's closed." I continued toward the front door anyway so I could hear it for myself. Yes, due to the pandemic the governor had issued an order on March 9, 2020 closing all nursing homes to visitors.

My sister Kathy had been a resident at the nursing home for over two years. Late-stage dementia had left her bedridden, unable to feed herself, or speak.

Before the pandemic, I arrived most days around five p.m. to feed her dinner. I loved my time giving her nourishment. Kathy seemed to enjoy each spoonful of pureed food and this made me happy because she had an appetite. I took my time as I shared stories of my day and fun times we had shared together. The best part was when she smiled.

I was overcome with sadness as I called Kathy's husband Bruce to let him know the nursing home was closed to visitors. Bruce is a wonderful, kind, caring man, and I was filled with gratitude every time I watched his caring of my sister and his unconditional love for her. I could not have asked for a better brother-in-law.

My sister was diagnosed with dementia around 2017. Before that I had noticed small changes but I wanted to ignore the forgetfulness, the repeating, and the lack of attention. Dementia slowly steals your loved one away from you and you cannot do anything about it. I had cried and mourned every little loss that I witnessed over the last few years.

A few days later, everything except essential businesses like grocery stores, drugstores, and gas stations closed as well. It was scary, confusing, and so unsettling as everyone's day-to-day routine was upended. Every day at dinnertime I was filled with sadness. Kathy is six years older than I. She had taken care of me when we were younger, and since she'd become ill I had been helping her. Being unable to do that made me feel so helpless.

Kathy had taught me to be strong, independent, and resilient. She never told me what to do but she always demonstrated these qualities which I observed and tried to emulate. No matter how challenging life got, when Kathy and I were together we were always laughing. We laughed until we could not talk and tears ran down our faces. Kathy knew me better than anyone else, and I would venture to say I knew the most about her too.

I had missed that companionship, but never so much as now, when the shadow of the pandemic loomed over me. I live alone, and the thought of being in the house by myself for a few weeks seemed devastating. Little did I know that "a few weeks" would turn into several months.

The grocery store opened at six a.m. to accommodate seniors. The first time I went to shop for food, I donned a makeshift mask from a folded pink bandana and two elastic bands. It was still dark as I drove out of the garage. I was shaking and scared as I gathered food and searched for paper products. When I got home there was a complete wipe-down of everything I touched.

I felt anxious and fearful as I listened to the news and realized how serious the pandemic was becoming every day. Since the biggest impact was to the senior community I was concerned for my sister, my friends, and myself.

I started walking just to be outside the house, but as usual I did too much too fast and after nine days I needed to take a rest so my shin splints could heal. After a few days I was back to my walking routine. Walking was a way for me to calm down, clear my racing mind, and feel refreshed. One morning while on my walk I recalled memories from a summer when I was a child. At that moment I realized I was going to be just fine. I had survived being alone and isolated before.

Imagination

It was late June 1956, and I was sitting alone in the bedroom I shared with Kathy. She was sixteen years old and I was ten. Something had happened the night before and my sister went to live with her best friend Pat's family. They already had a full house—in addition to Pat's parents, there were six kids and a grandfather—yet they were kind enough to take my sister in. Little did they know she would be there for six months.

The madness my father was experiencing due to an alcohol addiction had gotten the best of him and he took his rage out on my mother and my sister. I guess since I was the youngest he just ignored my existence.

I was told to stay in the bedroom. My crime was just being me. My mother brought me food, then would come collect the dishes. If I wanted to go to the bathroom, I had to get her attention to see if the coast was clear for me to leave my room. There were days my mother would let me leave and walk to the library. From there I would go to the park in the center of town and read, or just daydream. It was a very lonely time.

We lived in a four-family wood-framed apartment building. I remember looking out the only window in the bedroom, though there was not much to see. There was a three-car garage, which was not used because the structure was unstable. A four-foot barrel was positioned a distance from the garage. All newspapers, magazines, and other items that needed to be disposed of were put in the barrel. Once a week the landlord would set the items on fire. The whole process really scared me. To the right of the barrel was a wooden rectangular structure that housed two garbage cans. This was my view of the world. There was no watching television and there were no friends to play with. I missed my sister desperately each day.

I had a wild, unbridled imagination which was identified in my early childhood. I remember my mother talking to the doctor about my imaginary friend named January. The doctor assured her it was normal for a child with no playmates to create a friend. He said as my social circle expanded, I would no longer need January in my life.

By the time I was ten, January was long gone, but my imagination remained very active. I loved when there was enough money for my mom to purchase a copy of the magazine, *Calling All Girls*, for me. In one of the issues there was a chapter about ballet, with illustrations of the five basic positions. I wanted to be a ballerina, however, having no previous lessons, that future was out of reach. So I created a world in which I was a ballerina; I practiced every day and imagined my performance on stage.

I would dance to the songs on the radio or listen to my sister's records on her record player—tunes like "Rock Around the Clock" by Bill Haley and his Comets and "Sh-Boom" by The Crew Cuts. The upbeat music made me happy as I danced around the bedroom and forgot how alone I felt.

My future seemed dim that summer. The characters in the many books I read became my friends. I was transported to a happier time, where there was laughter and fun in life.

These memories triggered my ability to survive loneliness. I had done it that summer and I would do it again. My mind shifted back to the present day and my walk. I could feel a smile as I felt stronger in that moment. As I walked faster, my mind continued to race with memories and creative ideas of how I was going to handle a pandemic by myself. I knew I could do it because I remembered I had tools and skills that would help me flourish, no matter the circumstances.

Choices

After that epiphany, my survival techniques kicked into gear. First, I knew it was critical to make a plan on how I was going to survive the isolation.

Since I couldn't see anyone in person, I made a concerted effort to keep the lines of communication open. I contacted friends by phone and email. I wrote notecards to them as well, and got names of people in nursing homes who might like a card every few weeks.

I am so thankful for Zoom, webinars, and other social media connections that allowed me to participate in exercise classes, yoga, and Zumba sessions. All the physical activity made me feel stronger.

It is funny how once you put out certain energy things start to show up. Over the past year I have participated in a number of online programs. Some were free and others were being offered for a reduced rate. My daily schedule filled up with fun activities. Sometimes I had to make a decision which one to choose because I was overbooked!

I became very aware of how everything I did, said, or thought was based on my choice. I could be depressed, anxious, sad, and lonely, or I could be grateful, loved, creative, and positive. Most of the time I chose the latter.

I spent more time on my deck then any year before. I enjoyed gazing at the birds flapping their wings in the birdbath. I always stopped whatever I was doing and gave the hummingbirds my undivided attention when they came to visit. As the seasons changed, my only outside activities were grocery shopping and walking. In my warm cozy house, I rekindled my joy of reading novels.

I not only survived the holidays by myself, I made them into a happy occasion. I did this by cultivating a feeling of celebration and gratitude, even though I was alone. I used the Christmas china every day. I decorated the house inside and out. Twinkle lights, holiday music, and the smell of cinnamon just make me smile. I ordered prepared meals so I had something special to eat. Yes, the holidays were different but I made them the best they could be without others around me. By giving gratitude for all I had, I did not feel deprived.

Later in life Kathy and I often reflected on how blessed we felt to have experienced the trauma of growing up in a dysfunctional home, where alcoholism, being poor, being hungry, cold, and abused were the norm. It didn't happen overnight, but after years of workshops, journaling, therapy, reading, and prayer, we realized that through these experiences we were able to develop compassion, empathy, and forgiveness. We understood that the choices we made were critical to how our lives unfolded.

Of course, we did not always make the choice that from the outside world would look like a success, but it was the lessons along the way that we were grateful for. We were always learning and open to new thoughts and ideas.

Every choice I made resulted in a positive or negative reaction. Fortunately for me I made more choices that resulted in me feeling joy, happiness, and gratitude. Sometimes I chose to feel sorry for myself or lonely. The result of those decisions left me feeling down, sad, and hopeless. I would let those feelings bubble up and give them a little of my energy, then let them go. I get to choose which voices I want to hear in my head and I choose peace, hope, and love.

On January 8, 2021, my sister passed. I had not been able to touch her for ten months. I had not even seen her since September, when we had a fifteen-minute window visit. That isolation was overwhelming.

Kathy was intelligent, generous, beautiful, fun, energetic, and she loved life. She was my biggest cheerleader, my therapist, my shopping buddy, my mentor, my laughing partner, and my amazing big sister. She will always be close to my heart. I choose to remember all the happiness we shared.

ABOUT THE AUTHOR: Sheila Dunn lives in Connecticut. After her retirement from Hartford Financial she pursued many new interests, including obtaining her Master Garden Certification and becoming a Simple Abundance Close to Home Certified Workshop Leader. Sheila danced with CT Sun Senior Dance Team (Sunsationals) for eight years. They performed at the CT Sun Women's Basketball Games. She was a contributing author to the anthology, *Pathways to Vibrant Health & Well-Being,* published in 2014. She participates in many volunteer opportunities in her community, and is an active member of the Connecticut Renewal Team - Retired & Senior Volunteer Program Advisory Council.

Sheila Dunn
smdunn12@aol.com
860-461-3932

CHAPTER 19

Sailing Lessons
Kathy Sipple

"I am the master of my fate, I am the captain of my soul."
~ William Erest Henley, Invictus

First Mate

"A smooth sea never made a skilled sailor." ~ Franklin D. Roosevelt

Upon graduation from the University of Michigan in 1988 my computer programmer boyfriend's proposal of marriage, along with a marketing job offer at the same software development company, draws me to Milwaukee, Wisconsin. We sign a lease on an adorable vintage apartment with a view of Lake Michigan. We can take sailing lessons together, how romantic!

The first ripple of trouble begins when our employer files bankruptcy. We scramble to find new jobs while continuing to plan our big wedding that has taken on a life of its own as expectations build. It turns out that marriage—and sailing—both require a level of cooperation and communication beyond our current capabilities as a team. Just before our one-year anniversary my husband announces he wants a divorce. The one-sidedness of the decision is what hurts the most. It was not a discussion; instead, he has decided he doesn't love me and that our marriage was a mistake. He says he will be better off on his own.

Dry Dock

"A ship in the harbor is safe, but that's not what ships are built for." ~ William Shedd

Tell tales are pieces of yarn or fabric attached to a sail that provide information for sailors about how to adjust their sails. I had willfully ignored the "tells" about my marriage and my career that could have warned me. I had wanted to believe in the illusion of love more than I wanted to risk making waves by taking up space, making my voice heard. Now at age twenty-six I am living alone for the first time in my life, and I embrace it as an opportunity to turn my attention inward. I begin to see what a gift it is to reimagine my life on my own terms.

In my new tiny apartment, I begin to meditate regularly. I meet my Higher Self. She shows me a vision forty or so years from now. My blond hair is now snow white but my blue eyes are recognizable. They sparkle like mine, but are happier and wiser. She lives in a cooperative of some sort with a diverse group of people she loves and who love her. She is a trusted elder and has somehow been instrumental in bringing about this community perched next to a lake and surrounded by woods. She shares information about natural health and spiritual education with those who live here as well as occasional visitors who come to learn during their stay. I wake, excited to capture the vivid details in my journal before it fades. I nickname her "The Old Woman of the Woods."

I am grateful to have this powerful vision to guide me, though I have no idea how to get there.

I do sense that before recoupling, I need to become stronger, more fully myself. I have been too busy concerning myself with others' needs and expectations to reflect upon my own.

I reacquaint myself with my Inner Child. I listen to my body and realize she craves touch, so I schedule regular massages. She also wants to sing, make art, and spend time in nature. I also train my Inner Parent to take a more balanced approach toward her role. She will no longer get to dictate goals, but must take direction from the Inner Child and Higher Self too. I applaud her desire to track the goals in a log, though, as this will be useful feedback to know how we're doing.

My Higher Self gently nudges me to learn about herbs, read tarot cards, practice yoga, become a Reiki Master, study *A Course in Miracles* and Kabbalah.

My Adult Self is our Captain. She becomes skillful at integrating all the players with day-to-day requirements while not losing sight of Higher Self's long-term vision. She follows career opportunities that hold the most promise for growth and learning. She buys a house on her own, close to family but far away from any lakes where she can sail.

By age thirty-one I am ready to love—and sail—again. My little blue sailboat waits patiently, on a trailer in the driveway for a new adventure.

Setting Sail

"On a day when the wind is perfect, the sail just needs to open and the world is full of beauty." ~ Rumi

One June evening, after a four-hour drive, I am greeted by a gorgeous view of my beloved Lake Michigan in Michigan's Harbor Country. I have arrived early for a wedding rehearsal dinner and am enjoying a glass of wine on the restaurant's terrace. Aside from the bride and groom I don't know anyone very well. My loose plan is to go to the wedding the following day then continue on to Milwaukee and Chicago and spend the rest of the week visiting friends I haven't seen in a long time.

As I sip my wine, I realize weddings no longer trigger me. I am simply a guest at a wedding, not a "divorced woman with a failed marriage." I look up when a tall man approaches and asks if he may join my table. His name is John. He has driven from Chicago and is also early for the same rehearsal dinner. Over more wine, we share details about ourselves. The conversation flows easily. We continue talking after the rehearsal dinner and arrange to meet in the morning for breakfast before the wedding. We sit next to one another at the wedding too.

He is also taking the week ahead as vacation and has invited a houseful of friends and family to join him for the upcoming Fourth of July celebration at his lake house in the woods. He invites me to join them and I accept, saying I'll be there after I have visited with my own friends. Away from him for a few days, I reconsider, wondering if he had invited me just to be polite; however, a phone call from him to see if I'm still coming convinces me to go.

Our time together is magical; being with him feels like home. After a few years of dating long-distance and nightly phone conversations, I move north to Chicago to be with him. It melts my heart when John changes the ball bearings on the boat trailer and tows it himself to the lake house in Michigan for me. Though he is not a sailor, he knows how much I love it. He's a Libra, an air sign, and I'm a Cancer, a water sign—together we contain the elements to sail metaphorically together. When we marry, we keep the plan just between the two of us. The ceremony takes place in the snowy northern woods with only a minister, a witness, and our Black Labrador retriever.

A Shared Vision

"The voyage of the best ship is a zigzag line of a hundred tacks." ~ Ralph Waldo Emerson, Self-Reliance

We honeymoon at the same lake house where we first met and invite friends and family to join us to celebrate our marriage after the fact. I remind John about my vision of the Old Woman of the

Woods. There are elements of it that feel like what we are experiencing now—togetherness, nature, sharing. Yet it is also different—we are older but also we are not the hosts, paying for everything and making all the decisions alone. Instead the property is owned jointly and responsibilities shared. That part feels important. For now, we enjoy our good fortune and celebrate our new marriage with our guests.

In sailing, if your destination is upwind, it is impossible to sail directly there; instead you need to be able to tack, to shift the rudder and the sail one way and then the next while remaining fixed on an end destination. John and I communicate what we notice—changes in the wind—and decide together how and when to adjust our course. During our twenty-plus years together we navigate a move to a new state, downsizing, losing a business, bankruptcy, career changes, stock market crashes, health crises, deaths of loved ones, betrayals, and buying a business.

We work individually and as a couple to become more agile, more resilient in the face of emergencies and now want to help others feel more prepared and connected. John researches how to transition the business he has built into an employee stock ownership program. I start a timebank in which members trade time instead of money. One of the most popular offerings in the timebank is a sailing experience on Lake Michigan! The timebank member who owns the boat meets news friends and enjoys letting everyone take a turn at the helm. He receives maintenance help on the boat in return. It's a first step toward operating cooperatively.

Timebanking leads me to other interesting groups and projects. I join HUMANS (humans united in mutual aid networks). I visit the Venus Project in Florida, a new socioeconomic model utilizing science and technology. I attend Chicago's First Cooperative Economic Summit. I study Michael Tellinger's Ubuntu Movement and Transition Town. I attend Asset-Based Community Development

training at DePaul University in Chicago. I attend social permaculture training called Activating Cultural Emergence with Looby
Macnamara, Starhawk, and Jon Young in Oakland, California. I
feel like a busy bee collecting pollen for the hive, though the hive
isn't quite ready to receive it yet. Most people I talk to have a hard
time understanding what I'm doing.

The Horizon Nears

*"The sooner we learn to be jointly responsible, the easier the
sailing will be." ~ Ella Maillart*

It's March 2020 and we are in a global pandemic. I am fifty-three,
John almost sixty. Like most of the rest of the world, we are making
adjustments to our routine, including our work lives. My in-person
marketing training work comes to a halt and I am left with too much
time on my hands and missing connection and purpose as well as
a lack of income.

Marketing no longer holds my interest the way it once did, but
I have not integrated the new tools I have been learning about
into a career—to this point it has been more of a passion project. I
update my LinkedIn profile with some verbiage about "resilience"
and "regenerative economy," along with some of the things I've
been working on. Within weeks, my needed opportunity finds me!
Governance Alive in Washington D.C. is starting a training institute
(online due to covid-19) and they want marketing help to get them
up and running. They will be teaching various social technologies,
but will start with "Sociocracy," a term I learn translates to "deciding together."

I love what I learn about sociocracy and their approach, which
involves making sure every voice is heard and also checking in with
the body's wisdom to determine if a proposal has inner consent. I
enroll as a student in the training and immediately begin to use what
I am learning to conduct more effective meetings. The teams I have

been trying to lead are finally "flocking together" and don't need me to lead them, merely to facilitate. This feels like the missing piece I have needed to activate great ideas into successful projects.

Participants in my courses tend to be conscious evolutionaries, sustainability professionals, blockchain companies, creative types, and some even specifically work with intentional communities! We learn from one another in our monthly study groups. I begin to assist with training the beginner Sociocracy course. I can't get enough of it!

Now I am halfway through my credentialed program toward becoming a Certified Sociocracy Facilitator and Consultant, and will finish my advanced training in 2022. By the time I reach that not-so-distant shore of my vision I'm more confident than ever that I will know just what to do!

ABOUT THE AUTHOR: Kathy Sipple is available to help communities build resilience through social technology, climate action, timebanking and permaculture. She is a Sociocracy Facilitator-in-training and is working on a book, *Healing Earth Together*, expected to be published in 2021. The book will serve as a guide for communities to address environmental and social justice issues while enriching the quality of life. Sipple holds a degree in Economics from the University of Michigan and is a member of Mensa. She lives in Valparaiso, Indiana—the "Vale of Paradise"—with her husband John and their black Lab, Bodhi.

Kathy Sipple
CoThrive Community
kathysipple.com
kathy@kathysipple.com
219-405-9482

CHAPTER 20

Navigating Realms

Nora Yolles Young

We are spirit beings having a human experience. You are not here on the surface of this planetary body twirling through space to be safe. You are here to live life *on purpose*. Sure, your body will die someday. It could be in five minutes from now, or many years in the future. Since we know the inevitable, isn't it time to really sink our teeth into what it is to be intentional about living this present life?

More than anything else in this world, I want to live life full-on, no holds barred. Each day, I take a firm step forward, and life happens; I take it in, rinse, and repeat. And that is what living on purpose is for me: mindfully becoming clear, conscious, and aware of my desire to do this thing with intention, passion, and gusto. It is about learning how to nimbly navigate and straddle that space between the living, Earthly realm and the subtle, non-physical realm of spirit. In fact, living my purpose is the natural byproduct of the lessons and gifts I received through my experiences with and around the portal of death.

My professional work is designed to help people align with living their lives on purpose. I do this by working through and within their consciousness to help them move the often unconscious, uncomfortable, and traumatic memories, thoughts, and beliefs into the light of day, where it can be shifted and healed in ways that empower and create a sense of personal sovereignty. It's fun, exciting work, and each session with a client or group is like a new adventure unfolding in the moment. It is my mission and activism.

I've always been fascinated by death—not in a macabre, creepy way, but in a fascinated, curious kind of way (you can be the judge of all that). When I was five, a man riding a motorcycle through our peaceful, magnolia-lined, historic Victorian neighborhood an hour and a half east of Houston was hit at an intersection by a box truck. I was at home when the accident happened and heard the motorcyclist's screams merge with the sounds of impact. It was an unmistakably horrific cacophony of destiny; timing, metal, velocity, and human frailty together in one life-ending moment. My house was a full block and a half away, but it was as if I were right there. I felt deeply interconnected to what was happening.

I remember asking Rosey, our witchy babysitter with a tight salt-and-pepper bun and frequent grin of pointy tooth nubs—the only dentition that remained in her mouth after a lifetime of Coca-Cola abuse. Rosey had heard the crash too, and solemnly told us kids to wait on the porch while she investigated. We watched her slight frame march off down the block and saw the box truck askew in the middle of the sleepy, sun-dappled street. The distance was too far to catch sight of the man on the ground, but his moans reverberated through the heavy midday Texas heat.

There was an imposing sense of doom in the air, so palpable it could be felt in the bones. My soul knew, even at that young age, that the spirit realm was calling back one of their own.

My knowing was confirmed when Rosey returned to the porch, shook her head at me, and said there was nothing anyone could do. My body reacted with panic. *What do you mean, nothing we can do? We have to do something!* I puffed my determined kid-self up and boldly started to head in that direction.

I asked Rosey, "Is he going to die?"

"I don't know," she replied, "but it does not look good. The ambulance has not even arrived and he really needs help." Then Rosey gave me a pointed look and told me this was for adults only. Part of me wanted to see and the rest of me was afraid of what I would find.

I imagined a man in a red jacket and jeans, pinned underneath the front tire of a giant truck, slowly dying alone as helpless observers watched. I don't actually know if that was the scene, because I never saw it, yet the significance remains. It was a potent moment for my young soul to acknowledge.

I later asked my parents, and though they didn't know anything about it I knew in my heart that the man on the motorcycle had indeed died. Though the event saddened me; I wasn't scared; in fact, it triggered an even deeper interest in death. My mom, who comes from a lineage of female hobby spiritualists, liked to get the gals together and have seances to communicate with past loved ones. I loved the stories Mom told me about her experiences and visitations with spirit; they impacted my child's mind and made me long for experiences of my own. I even had a purple booklet of ghost facts and stories that I loved to carry around and show people. It was my little badge of honor.

This fascination (maybe slight obsession) with death wasn't about the end of life, but how it impacted it. It was deeply interwoven into my understanding of being alive in these earthly bodies, and that stuff that animates us. Our lifeforce enters as we arrive, then exits our bodies once the portal of life opens to take us home. What my soul longed to know is how we can have a good life that openly embraces our spiritual selves in a non-compartmentalized, nonreligious, non-stigmatizing way—a way that feels true to the essence of my being. My work shows people how to do that. It provides that perfect combination of soul realm and human realm all blended into one. Over time I discovered that my fascination with death was actually my unconscious drive to work with spirit while bringing people to their own innate soul wisdom as a type of guidance while here on Earth.

I had no way of knowing how to do this, no template to follow, but life continued to offer opportunities to explore. In college, I fell in love with archeology, and especially bones. This was my way of scratching that soul realm yearning, and it satiated my needs for years. From 1994 to 2003, I worked as an archaeologist either as a student or a contract archaeologist. I got to excavate burial chambers and long-forgotten burial sites. My sensitivity to the spirit realm would pop in as reminders to be honoring and reverent of my work when handling human remains; these reminders were experienced as electric pulses or shocks coming directly from the bones, and they only happened when I was not very intentional with my work.

Then, in 2000, my father was diagnosed with terminal, metastatic kidney cancer. Receiving the call that Dad had a golf-ball-sized tumor in his brain was the moment my life tilted on its axis. He was going into surgery the following morning, so I hurriedly packed a bag and caught a flight from San Francisco, where I was in my first semester of grad school studying palliative care, to Hawaii. (We'd moved from Texas back to Hawaii, the place of my birth, when I was six). I arrived at Queens Medical Center in Honolulu the next day as he was being wheeled out of post-surgical recovery. I remember the flood of grief that I felt seeing him, and worried that our time together might be limited. It was an unfamiliar emotion, a heart hurt more excruciating than anything I'd ever known. I crawled into the hospital bed with him and did everything I could to hold his life inside his body. I held him and wailed.

Dad would live with his illness for the next two and a half years, during which he received exhaustive treatments and surgeries. It was an emotional roller coaster ride for all involved, including me, but my connection with the spirit realm had prepared me in some way for his death. In fact, something innate blossomed in me through this process.

By the spring of 2003 it was clear that he was really going downhill. Also clear was my mission: to support his spiritual journey through this transition. Dad and I devised a plan: he would let me know when it was "time," and I would hop on a plane from California and be there with him for as long as he needed. He understood that this meant his death, which, of course, was really tough for him to articulate.

When that call came, I worked out my life to facilitate a flexible timeframe and flew to Maui to help my dad do this dying thing. Thankfully, he also had a lot of support from his wife and Hospice Maui. When I arrived he was still walking around, but over the course of the month I was there he would quickly move to a walker, a wheelchair, and, finally, a hospital bed. He was going into a more and more internal state. Just before his hospital bed arrived, I remember snuggling with him and asking how he was doing. Though he replied, "Fine," something inside of me knew I had to rattle the cage a little. "Oh really?" I said, "Because I thought you were dying? That's why I flew out here." This was not said to make him feel bad. It was to bring up the opportunity to talk about what was really happening.

Then he said, "Sometimes I like to pretend."

I asked, "How does it feel to know you are dying?"

"I don't like it! And I don't know how to do it."

"I get it. It sucks! You don't have to know how to die. Your body does. Let your body lead. Just lean in. It's a perfectly natural thing."

That was the conversation that I knew I had to have with him. As he continued to decline, I had the opportunity to shave him, to help him with his bodily functions, and keep him company. We all so lovingly held space for him in this sacred time. It required so much letting go on his part and he did it with such grace.

The morning that his body released his soul energy, I was napping on the couch in the living room. The house was full of people and we'd held vigil all night. In my dream state, I saw smokey energy tendrils traveling down the hallway. I understood this to be his soul's energy leaving the house. I arose in my dream and opened the door for the soul energy to leave and watched it slowly float upward. Then my conscious self jerked awake and I ran to his room. His body was still breathing but it was not going to be long. His heart stopped at 4:14 a.m. (HST) on June 2, 2003.

My twin brother and I had planned to go to our favorite beach to swim once he'd passed. That morning, as the sun rose over the south side of Maui, my father's soul energy was palpable. It was everywhere and so joyful and free. We'd predetermined that red cardinals would be how his soul energy would communicate his presence, and that morning we were inundated with them, flying in a sacred celebration above us as we walked the beach path.

The whole family felt him around us all day, then he was gone. Two weeks after he passed he visited me in a vivid dream and let me know he was "fueling up his pod and heading out on a long journey and would be away for a while." He also said he was okay, and not to worry about him.

Later in 2011, while I was the student demo for my past life regression training, my father delivered soul-to-soul communication about the reason he had died. He used the words, "I took one for the team." He showed me that we all agreed to play these parts and that he'd made this agreement before entering his life as Milton Yolles. He owned all of it. He also made it clear that he would be present to support me with my work every step of the way as part of my healing team from the other side.

Flash forward ten years, to 2021. My relationship with my father has evolved far beyond what even I had imagined. I feel his energy and support in everything I do. Thinking about my dad now is more like thinking about a spiritual guide. I still grieve for his human self. I miss our lunches, the sound of his voice, his wit, and the feeling of his hugs. Oh, do I miss those! But through his life, and the powerful life lesson of his exit from this physical world, I was gifted more clarity and understanding about my soul purpose and work: that I am a living bridge between the spirit and human realms. I help people become their own bridge when they're ready. And I know many of you reading this now are indeed ready, so come on in, the water's fine!

ABOUT THE AUTHOR: Nora Yolles Young B.C.H. C.I., LBL® has a Bachelor of Arts degree in Human Origins and Prehistory from The University of Redlands, Johnston Center. She was born and raised in Hawaii, and now lives with her husband and two children in central North Carolina. Certain that she is living her soul purpose, she considers her work as a board-certified hypnotherapist, integrative consciousness coach, and certifying transpersonal spiritual hypnotherapy and regression instructor to be her art and craft. She is client-centered in her approach and blends her expertise and understanding of people throughout the ages, human cultures, and consciousness into innovative healing tools in her practice, groups, training, lectures, and publications.

Nora Yolles Young
Young Hypnotherapy
YoungHypnotherapy. com
info.younghypno@gmail.com
919-742-0790

About the Authors

**Are you inspired by the stories in this book?
Let the authors know.**

**See the contact information at the end of each chapter
and reach out to them.**

They'd love to hear from you!

Author Rights & Disclaimer

*Each author in this book retains the copyright and all inherent
rights to their individual chapter. Their stories are printed herein
with each author's permission.*

*Each author is responsible for the individual opinions expressed
through their words. Powerful You! Publishing bears no responsibility for the content of the stories by these authors.*

Acknowledgements & Gratitude

We are forever grateful for the many beautiful and loving individuals who grace our lives. We're especially happy and grateful for our circle that continues to grow and for the gifts they each bestow.

To the authors of this book, we honor, love, and admire you. Your openness with your stories exemplifies your passion for assisting individuals in their lives, and your personal resilience and courage light the way for us to be braver in our own lives. Thank you for sharing this journey with us. We are honored.

Our editor Dana Micheli: Your intuition, sense of humor, creativity, and willingness are a perfect fit to get to the heart of the stories. We appreciate our partnership and friendship, and we love you.

Our training team: AmondaRose Igoe, Kathy Sipple, Karen Flaherty, and Francine Sinclair—your expertise, big hearts, and guidance are so helpful for our authors. We love and appreciate each of you.

Moira Forsythe – We are honored to share this experience with you, and we appreciate your passion and mission to assist individuals on their infinite journey.

There are many beautiful souls who we gratefully call our tribe and our family who offer guidance, expertise, love, and support! You've helped make us better humans.

Above all, we are grateful for the Divine Spirit that flows through us each day providing continued blessings, lessons, and opportunities for growth, peace, and JOY!

Namaste` and Blessings, Love and Gratitude,
Sue Urda and Kathy Fyler
Publishers

About Sue Urda and Kathy Fyler

Sue and Kathy have been business partners since 1994. They have received many awards and accolades for their businesses over the years and continue to they love the work they do and the people they attract to work with. As publishers, they are honored to help people share their stories, passions, and lessons.

Their mission is to raise the vibration of people and the planet and to connect and empower women in their lives. Their calling has been years in the making 'forever' and is a gift from Spirit.

The strength of their partnership lies in their deep respect, love, and understanding of one another as well as their complementary skills and knowledge. Kathy is a technology enthusiast, web goddess, and freethinker. Sue is an author and speaker with a love of creative undertakings and great conversations. Their honor, love, and admiration for each other are boundless.

Together their energies combine to feed the flames of countless women who are seeking truth, empowerment, joy, peace, and connection with themselves, their own spirits, and other women. They believe we are all here in this lifetime to support and love of one another, and they are grateful to fulfill this purpose through their publishing company.

Connect with Sue and Kathy:

Powerful You! Publishing
powerfulyoupublishing.com
info@powerfulyou.com
239-280-0111

About Dr. Moira M. Forsythe

Dr. Moira M. Forsythe, ND, CPC, ELI-MP, CDLS, PPP is an iPEC certified professional leadership coach and naturopathic practitioner whose passion for empowering others to their best lives has been a central theme for her for over 35 years. Moira regularly lectures nationally and internationally to large groups on the topics of bioenergetics and lifestyle balance. Living above 8500 ft in a remote area of the Rocky Mountains gives her a unique perspective of what balance with the natural world can look, feel and be like.

In addition to the CPC, Moira holds professional certifications in Positive Psychology, Core Dynamics Leadership, Group Coaching, and Energy Leadership Coaching. She has led transition and empowerment Mastermind groups for entrepreneurs, women, and athletes for over 15 years. Her success with emerging entrepreneurs seeking to change the social culture of the world is making a difference around the globe.

Connect with Moira:

Dr. Moira M. Forsythe, ND, CPC, PPP
Executive Coach, Author, Speaker
Founder: Level 7 Coaching, Creative Leadership Systems
CreativeLeadershipSystems.com/CoachesThatCare.org
creativeleadershipsystems@gmail.com

Powerful You! Publishing
Sharing Wisdom ~ Shining Light

Are You Called to be an Author?

If you're like most people, you may find the prospect of writing a book daunting. Where to begin? How to proceed? No worries! We're here to help.

Whether you choose to contribute to an anthology or write your own book, we're here for you. We'll be your guiding light, professional consultant, and enthusiastic supporter. If you see yourself as an author partnering with a publishing company who has your best interest at heart and expertise to back it up, we'd be honored to be your publisher.

We provide personalized guidance through the writing and editing process, as well as many necessary tools for your success as an author. We offer complete publishing packages and our service is designed for a personal and optimal author experience.

We are committed to helping individuals express their voice and shine their light into the world. Are you ready to start your journey as an author? Do it with Powerful You! Publishing.

 Powerful You!
PUBLISHING
Sharing Wisdom ~ Shining Light

Powerful You! Publishing
239-280-0111
powerfulyoupublishing.com

Recommended Reading

Empowering Transformations for Women
Women Living Consciously
Journey to Joy
Pathways to Vibrant Health & Well-Being
Women Living Consciously Book II
Healthy, Abundant, and Wise
Keys to Conscious Business Growth
The Gifts of Grace & Gratitude
Heal Thy Self
Empower Your Life
Heart & Soul
The Beauty of Authenticity
WOKE
The Art and Truth of Transformation for Women

PURPOSE...

Feel your way through.
Breathe it in.

Live into it.